Shakespeare
A Beginner's Guide

ONEWORLD BEGINNER'S GUIDES combine an original, inventive, and engaging approach with expert analysis on subjects ranging from art and history to religion and politics, and everything in-between. Innovative and affordable, books in the series are perfect for anyone curious about the way the world works and the big ideas of our time.

Shakespeare
A Beginner's Guide

Ros King

A Oneworld Paperback Original

Published by Oneworld Publications 2011
Reprinted, 2021

Copyright © Ros King 2011

The right of Ros King to be identified as the Author
of this work has been asserted by her in accordance with the
Copyright, Designs and Patents Act 1988

ISBN 978-1-85168-789-3
eISBN 978-1-78074-048-5

Typeset by Jayvee, Trivandrum, India
Cover design by www.vaguelymemorable.com
Printed and bound in Great Britain by Clays Ltd, Elcograf S.p.A.

Oneworld Publications
10 Bloomsbury Street
London WC1B 3SR

Stay up to date with the latest books,
special offers, and exclusive content from
Oneworld with our newsletter

Sign up on our website
oneworld-publications.com

For Tam and Ray

Contents

Acknowledgements

My thanks go to Marsha Filion at Oneworld for first suggesting and then helping to shape this project, and to Rachel Beaumont, for her patience and immensely helpful editorial suggestions. I am grateful too to the press's anonymous reader, to Bella Millett who read the manuscript at its final stage, and to countless students and actors whose responses to these ideas over the years have helped me refine and develop them.

Introduction: Why Shakespeare?

> Yet, do thy worst, old Time. Despite thy wrong,
> My love shall in my verse ever live young.
>
> (Sonnet 19)

Shakespeare's plays and poems have survived both in print and on the stage for four hundred and fifty years. He is probably the most performed and reprinted poet and dramatist of all time. More than that, his work has encouraged constant quotation, reinvention, reinterpretation, translation, and rewriting since it first appeared; and not just in England or in Britain but across the world. My aim in writing this book is to explore some of the reasons for this, and also the reasons why, for many people, 'Shakespeare' is a daunting hill to climb. This book is for people who enjoy Shakespeare and want to think about the reasons for that. It is also for people who have been put off him, by reputation or through the dreariness of having to mug up on selected scenes for the purposes of school examinations. I want to consider the plays and poems for their sensory and emotional qualities – for pace and movement, sound and rhythm – and for the social, ethical problems they present.

The cultural significance of Shakespeare means that he is too important to be left to the experts. And it is not the job of this book to give easy answers for 'beginners'. Any attempt to do so would be to falsify his work and, paradoxically, would make it appear *more* rather than less difficult. I hope that I can persuade readers not to run from the difficulties they will find, or to dismiss them as simply the product of a different time or an archaic and outdated language. Rather they should be embraced as deliberate features of the language that demand our emotional response, and create the sense of human interaction that speaks to us across centuries despite enormous cultural changes. I am trying to describe how the plays work, not to nail down what they mean.

My aim is to offer observations on the ways Shakespeare structures his plays, and techniques for approaching his language. Throughout, I shall be using and demonstrating a multi-dimensional approach, which combines literary analysis, cultural history, and performance history, with practical performance considerations, and audience/reader responses. There are therefore a number of case studies of individual plays and poems dotted through the book; these should be read as demonstrations of dramaturgical close-reading techniques that can also be applied to other works by Shakespeare. It is not my intention to provide plot summaries or introductions for each of the plays in the canon, since these are readily available elsewhere.

In fact, even very young beginners can be experts in the issues that are explored in the action of these plays. Primary school children understand perfectly the kinds of parent–child and sibling relationships shown in *King Lear*. They enjoy the insults that Lear's loyal servant Kent, disguised as Caius, throws at the mealy-mouthed Oswald, and they relish the horror of the eye-gouging scene, all while being able to relate these events thoughtfully to their own experience of bullying in the playground. They also instantly recognise that the main story is a version of *Cinderella* – not feeling, as an adult might, that this could devalue a work revered as one of the greatest classics of world literature.

I hope to show that the plays are not well served by teaching, criticism, or performance that offers 'right' answers – but that does not mean that there are no wrong answers. We are of course free to make any personal and private interpretation of Shakespeare that we like. But if we wish to make those interpretations public we need to judge their validity. Has our interpretation done justice to the play's structure, or has it closed it down? Are we offering our readers and audiences a rich or a restricted version of the play? This book will offer tools to help readers tell the difference. It will also debunk a number of myths, both about Shakespeare as a person and a writer and about the received meanings of some key plays. And it will place Shakespeare's career and works in the context of play-writing and play-production in late sixteenth- and early seventeenth-century London.

Shakespeare has become a surer livelihood for the countless theatre companies and film-makers who now perform him than most still-living playwrights. He is also relied upon to breathe life into less compelling work by politicians, writers, copy-editors, and advertising agents, who quote him, frequently without fully understanding the implications of what they are saying. When the former British Prime Minister Margaret Thatcher quoted 'Shakespeare' as saying 'to thine own self be true ... Thou canst not then be false to any man' (*Hamlet*, 1.3.78–80) she seemed blissfully unaware that the words are not a product of Shakespeare's genius or knowledge of human nature. Rather, they constitute a familiar proverbial saying, chosen by the dramatist to be spoken by the character Polonius, a prime minister and skilful politician in a corrupted court.

A few scenes after he speaks these lines (and here is where Shakespeare's brilliance as a dramatist lies), we will see him with one Reynaldo, a shadowy character who appears in no other scene in the play. He orders Reynaldo to follow his son to Paris and to spy on him, not stinting to play a few dirty tricks if necessary to get information. We may laugh at Polonius's apparently harmless forgetfulness in this scene, and enjoy being insiders in his scheme, but the effect is chilling. This little scene, too often cut in performance, demonstrates that surveillance is normal in this court. Twice in the course of the play, Polonius will conceal himself as a spy. It is this that gets him killed. The irony of Shakespeare's choice of proverb is that as spymaster, Polonius is truest to himself and to the king his master when he is most *un*true to others. For someone in Mrs Thatcher's position, quoting this character ought to be regarded as distinctly risky. The fact that no one either on her own side before she made the speech, or on the opposition benches afterwards, thought to remark on this unfortunate choice of erudition simply demonstrates our pressing need to rethink our approach to drama. Shakespeare's plays aren't collections of aphorisms for moral instruction; they don't tell his audiences what to think. Instead, the arrangement of his plays – the way in which he plots his storylines, and the parallels, the puns, and the echoes that run through them – encourages his audiences and readers to question what they hear and see.

Shakespeare's time and place

Shakespeare was writing at a very difficult period in English history. The state religion changed numerous times in his and his parents' lifetimes, not only back and forth between Catholicism and reformed religion, but between different shades of reformation. The reign of Elizabeth I, from 1558 to 1603, was longer than that of any other English monarch with the exception of Victoria and Elizabeth II. But it was far from secure. The ever-present threat of invasion came to a head in 1588 with the Spanish Armada, and again, though less famously, in 1599. Factions at court jockeyed for influence over the queen, while economic and religious unrest in the country both caused and was prompted by state repression.

We can be sure from the multitude of conflicting texts on religion and politics that still survive from that period that not all Elizabethans thought the same way. Social change would be impossible if societies were monolithic, and the period saw the beginnings of ideas and institutions that, for better or worse, have come to shape the modern world. Some hundred years before the formation of the Bank of England Shakespeare and his father were money-lenders, a role vital to the functioning of capitalism; a number of his business associates were members of the Virginia Company, formed to plant colonies in north America; Elizabethans were consciously trying to develop both their standards of manufacture and their capacity for trade. It was also a time that valued argument, that saw the beginning of the scientific, rational method of thought, and which had seen so many rigidly imposed religious changes in forty years that the only pragmatic way forward was to embrace a more secular politics.

Despite a hardening by the turn of the century of the idea that the monarch enjoyed divine right, there was an established tradition in England that he or she governed by counsel. Provided the subject was suitably handled, it could be useful to hear difficult matters discussed, whether in serious contexts such as sermons, or university disputations – the formal oratorical method whereby students progressed in their degrees – or in the playful forum of dramatic entertainment. It was the context and the treatment more than the content that determined whether any particular speech or play was regarded as seditious.

In the course of this book, we will see that the storylines for Shakespeare's plays are almost invariably borrowed from existing stories. But his practice of putting multiple stories together in ways that cross geographical time and space, using closely observed and vividly drawn characters to stage conflict and differences of opinion, creates complexity, which throws those opinions into question. Shakespeare's history plays compress or expand the course of historical events, and are filled with anachronisms. Non-historical characters such as the Bastard in *King John*, or even Queen Margaret who, though real enough, was historically not present in any of the scenes in which she appears in *Richard III*, comment freely, sometimes outrageously, on the action.

Thus, under the guise of fantasy, or remote or ahistorical history, Shakespeare is able to explore social and political problems, which would otherwise be forbidden to him. He can also tap in to the *potential* of human behaviour, rather than being bound by historically specific conventions. It is this that both enables him safely to explore some of the hot political issues of his time, and leaves the door open for later generations to read the plays in the light of later experience, both personal and cultural.

Theatre and the world

The concept that 'All the world's a stage/And all the men and women merely players' was already ancient when Shakespeare penned that line for the melancholy traveller Jacques in *As You Like It* (2.7.139–40). The idea that the gods look down and observe the actions of men as a play, and that different individuals or sections of society can also look at each other in this way, is found repeatedly in classical Greek and Roman literature, which in turn supplied a ready image to be employed in the literature of Shakespeare's time.

Thus, in a poem contemplating the perils of greatness, Shakespeare's contemporary, John Davies of Hereford, a moral poet and teacher of handwriting to the nobility, compares his own 'mean' or middle station in life to being a spectator in a theatre, leaning on a pillar – then often regarded as a symbol of inner strength or fortitude – amongst a crowd or 'press' of people in the middle gallery:

... like a looker on a tragedy
Within the middle room, among the mean,
I see the fall of state and majesty
While 'mongst the press t'a pillar sure I lean;
So see I others' sorrows with delight,
Though others' sorrows do but make me sad;
But plagues to see, which on our selves might light,
Free from their fall, makes nature, grieving, glad.

(John Davies, *Wit's Pilgrimage*, 1605)

Davies pits his own thoughts and feelings against those he sees enacted on the stage. He is probably correct; we enjoy watching misfortune when it reinforces our own sense of security. We feel empathy for these 'people' playing out their lives in front of us, even though we know it is a fiction; we watch the actors present the characters, yet the act of watching encourages us to think about what we would do in a similar situation; we are sad while knowing that we have no reason to be sad about a fiction, even one based on true events; we might sympathise with the characters while simultaneously appraising the actor's skill. We will be engaged by the story; we may even be implicated in it, when villains like Richard, Duke of Gloucester in *Richard III* or Iago in *Othello* take us into their confidence and spark our enjoyment in their plots and murders. At the same time, that constant physical consciousness of ourselves (the pressure of the pillar) reminds us that our lives are separate from what we see depicted, and enables us to maintain a sceptical distance. This ambivalence is important, and distinguishes the theatrical experience on the stage from theatrics in everyday life, where, for example, we might be swept along for real by a demagogue's oratory, becoming pawns in that individual's personal ambitions.

Playacting is nevertheless an intrinsic part of being human. Even within minutes of being born, babies are able to interact with other humans by mimicking their facial movements, frowning or smiling, and particularly, it seems, sticking out the tongue. As the child grows, this predisposition to imitation becomes conscious playfulness, and delight in games of make-believe. And yet because it is fiction, and therefore easily categorised as falsehood, playacting poses a moral problem. It straddles a fault-line in moral philosophy and human behaviour. On the one hand it is a mechanism for learning about the world, and for making our societies work. On the other, it can be seen as both coercive – a tool for social constraint, or behaving in the 'right' way – and subversive, immoral, and duplicitous. Shakespeare exploits these tensions to the full.

Case study: *The Tempest*

All Shakespeare's plays – even his English history plays – are set in a kind of nowhere-land outside geo-historical time and space. Sometimes this place amounts to pure fantasy – like the island in *The Tempest*, which is supposed to be somewhere in the Mediterranean between Naples and Tunisia but is simultane-ously an island in the Caribbean. Inspired by accounts of a shipwreck which took place off the coast of Bermuda in 1610, and by travellers' tales from exotic places beyond Europe, the island is peopled by strange creatures and spirits, who have been brought into subjection by the magus Prospero, the exiled Duke of Milan. The play's action concerns Prospero's revenge on his usurping brother, Antonio, who is travelling with the King of Naples when their boat comes within reach of the island. With the assistance of his slave spirit Ariel, Prospero whips up a magic storm, which apparently wrecks the boat, scattering the courtiers at different points round the island.

The fantasy island and its illusionary storm, quite isolated from the 'real' world, becomes the ideal place for a political exile, his spirit slaves, and a motley selection of shipwreck survivors from all social classes to play out conflicting ideas of power and of government. The king's brother, assisted by Antonio, plots an assassination, apparently not considering the futility of doing so when they are stranded far from the kingdom he wants to inherit; Prospero's slave, the monster Caliban, is only too ready to assist the king's butler in his attempt to become lord of the island, though all they achieve is to end up in a bog reeking of horse piss; the king's chief adviser, meanwhile, waxes lyrical on the beauty of the island and the social benefits of a utopian republicanism. Since the characters are so unaware of what is happening to them, Shakespeare is able to present both the violence and the impractical idealism with an undercurrent of humour, encouraging our critical and amused dissent from most of the opinions expressed. All the characters are shown to have their blind spots and weaknesses.

The play is also a love story between Prospero's daughter and the king's son, and an apparent tale of reconciliation; Prospero, his daughter, and the other Europeans all go home, and the island is left to its original inhabitant, Caliban. Importantly, though, the end is no fairy tale: difficulties still seethe under the surface, and Prospero still loathes his brother. Caliban vows to seek for grace, now he is about to be alone in his island kingdom; yet the beautiful young Miranda, Prospero's daughter, playing her young prince at chess, lovingly excuses what she thinks is his cheating at the game with the worrying jest that were he to 'wrangle' for a 'score of kingdoms', she would 'call it fair play' (*The Tempest*, 5.1.174–5). One can only speculate on how they will rule once they inherit the throne.

Thus a play written at the very beginnings of the European colonial enterprise can still speak to us beyond the end of that process. One of the most memorable recent productions seen in England was from the Baxter Theatre in South Africa, and drew on the country's experience of having a brutal colonial past brought to a flawed and difficult present through a determined process of 'peace and reconciliation'. The production used vivid tribal spirit dances to conjure the magical otherness of the island, and presented the king's party in nineteenth-century European dress. The dignity of an aged African Caliban (John Kani) leaning on his crutches as he turned to face his future as a free man at the end of the play was a powerfully evocative image of the issues, embodied in the actual history of the actor, as a veteran of apartheid South Africa. Shakespeare could never have conceived that production, yet it captured both the social and political dynamics of the play, and allowed the performers to express a truth about themselves. As a result it communicated powerfully with its audiences.

The way Shakespeare structures his plays, with multiple characters being put through variations on the same story, and making different choices, combined with his use of word-play and pun, poses ethical questions concerning human social inter-action. This is the reason why the plays are not limited by the culture of his own period. They are open systems, inviting input from their audiences. Their nuanced complexity, created through their language and structure, makes them rewatchable, rereadable, reinterpretable; we notice different things on each repeated encounter; they appeal differently at different stages in our lives and to different cultures and periods. And that is why this book will be about structures and processes, not meanings.

1

Who, and what, is Shakespeare?

'I am I, howe'er I was begot'
(*King John*, 1.1.175)

On 26 April 1564 a christening took place in Holy Trinity, the parish church of Stratford-upon-Avon. The entry written in Latin in the parish baptismal records states: William, son of John Shakespeare. The boy's birthday is not stated, but since christenings commonly took place within a few days of a child's birth, and since this child would later come to be regarded as England's national poet, the feast day of St George, England's national saint, has seemed, to some, too convenient a date to miss. April 23rd has therefore been celebrated as William's birthday ever since he became a national treasure in the later eighteenth century, although there is in fact no firm evidence for that date.

St George, the middle-eastern dragon-slayer of legend, is perhaps a surprising choice for English patron saint. In contrast, the story of William's life and death – a classic tale of talent combined with hard work – has sometimes seemed too ordinary for a poet of such stature. By dint of a serviceable education mostly in Latin in the local grammar school, a gift both for human observation and for business, and a startlingly good ear, this boy from the 'middling sort' (the son of a glove maker, wool dealer, and small town official) became a notable success in both the commercial and court theatre of his time. Again, the school part of this story is an assumption since the records of enrolment for the King Edward VI grammar school at Stratford no longer exist, but the alderman's son would have been entitled to a place, and the plays contain no more, and also no less knowledge of classical literature than that to which he would have been exposed as a pupil in a competent grammar school of the period.

This life trajectory is rather inspiring. But it threatens the very idea of the British class structure. Accordingly, since Victorian times, there has always been someone who will claim that William Shakespeare from Stratford was only the front man for some aristocrat who wished to hide a passion for popular theatre and writing: Edward de Vere, Earl of Oxford; Francis, Lord Bacon; Christopher Marlowe; even Queen Elizabeth herself have been touted as candidates – despite the fact that all but Bacon were dead long before some of the sources for the later plays appeared, and Bacon's acknowledged work bears no resemblance to the Shakespeare canon.

Shakespeare, the married man

The next set of dates in the records raises some equally doubtful matters. On 27 November 1582, the clerk to the court of the Bishop of Worcester recorded in Latin the grant of a special licence for a marriage between William Shaxpere and Anne Whateley of Temple Grafton. Along with a number of other names in the register, Anne's was mistaken by the clerk who wrote the entry. He should have written the name Hathaway but his confusion probably occurred because that day he had been dealing with a legal case concerning one William Whateley. The next day, two close friends of the bride's family stood surety for the sum of £40 in a marriage bond vouching for the legality of the proposed union between 'William Shagspere' and 'Anne Hathwey' of 'Stratford'. Six months later a daughter was born to the couple; Susanna Shakespeare was christened on 26 May 1583. Anne was therefore already three months pregnant when she walked up the aisle.

Normally a marriage ceremony would take place after the calling of the banns – which asked for information regarding any impediment to the marriage – on three consecutive Sundays or holy days. Canon law, however, demanded that no banns could be called between Advent Sunday (which that year fell on 2 December) and the Octave of Epiphany (13 January). For whatever reason, William and Anne had clearly run out of time for a marriage before Christmas. The special licence was therefore necessary because of the time of year, and also because William was still a minor.

Judging by the age of sixty-seven given on Anne's tombstone in 1623 – although tombstones are not always reliable – she was eight years older than her husband. Temple Grafton, where the incumbent was known to be an unreliable adherent to the old religion, and not allowed to solemnise marriages, has also caused problems. But we do not know where the marriage ceremony itself took place, and it is possible that Anne had been living in that hamlet at the time of the licence, just three and a half miles from the family home in Shottery.

These incomplete facts have caused endless salacious speculation: he married her because he had to; she was 'on the shelf'; they weren't happy; as soon as his twins Judith and Hamnet were born early in 1585, he left her and the screaming family in the country to go to live as an actor in London; and perhaps most famously, as supposed proof of all that, he left her in his will only the 'second best' bed.

Elizabethan marriage practice was not however identical with ours. It was perfectly acceptable for couples to have sex before marriage provided they were betrothed, or had gone through a simple exchange of vows before witnesses – *per verba de praesenti*. It was the betrothal that formed the legally binding agreement and which sorted out the financial arrangements between the families.

Shakespeare may also not have been as absent a father figure as has been supposed – at least not once he was established as a writer. The City authorities closed the London theatres whenever plague gave them the grounds for doing so. The acting companies would go on the road on these occasions, as they did in any case for two months every summer. Touring is not conducive to writing and Shakespeare may well have taken the opportunity to go home, both to write and to look after his property. He maintained myriad financial dealings in Stratford, including rights to tithes and rental income, and like his father, he was also engaged in lending money at interest, although unlike his father, he was never prosecuted for usury – lending money at more than ten per cent. But however he made his money, he was able to buy and refurbish New Place, the second-largest house in Stratford, as early as 1597, when he was just thirty-four. When in London, he seems to have preferred to live in rented rooms. The property he later bought in Blackfriars seems to have been an investment rather than a home.

Shakespeare's will is remarkable for the care with which he bequeaths his estate to his family, aiming to keep it intact down the generations, although the lack of surviving grandchildren thwarted this ambition. Susanna, who was his executor, along with her husband, was also the residuary legatee. Judith had made what Shakespeare probably regarded as a risky match; her husband had been called before the local Stratford church bawdy courts for fornication. Shakespeare's will therefore seems to have been altered in the light of her wedding to ensure that her portion would be safeguarded from any attempt by her husband to sell it. Until the Married Woman's Property Act of 1882, married women had no legal control over their own fortunes; their property belonged to their husbands. William thus used his will to circumvent the law.

Anne, meanwhile, was provided for as a matter of course, taking the dowager's right to live in the family home during her lifetime. In prestigious New Place, the second best bed would probably have been the bed that she and William had shared as husband and wife – the best bed being reserved to impress visitors. The will, as appropriate, is couched in formal and conventional legalese. But this bequest might suggest sentiment. And while it is always inadvisable to take literary texts as evidence for autobiography, Sonnet 145 does seem to play on her name:

> Those lips that Love's own hand did make,
> Breathed forth the sound that said 'I hate'
> To me that languished for her sake;
> But when she saw my woeful state
> ...
> 'I hate' she altered with an end
> That followed it as gentle day
> Doth follow night ...
>> 'I hate' from hate away she threw,
>> And saved my life, saying 'not you'.

Hate away, Hathaway; 'I hate not you'.

Apprentice, poacher, or schoolmaster in the country?

All these documentary facts about a middle-class Elizabethan life are open to varying interpretation, but details of Shakespeare's early career and particularly the means whereby he gained entry to his profession as an actor and writer are even less certain.

His father, John Shakespeare, may have had financial difficulties that forced William to leave school early. He certainly did not go on to university, which otherwise he might have expected to do at the age of sixteen, and it is possible that he was briefly apprenticed in his father's business. The old story that Shakespeare was forced to flee to London because he was caught poaching Sir Thomas Lucy's deer in Charlecote (or perhaps Fulbroke) park near Stratford has never quite gone away, although it can have absolutely nothing to do with how he managed to break in to a career in the theatre and make a living as a dramatist.

The story told by the gossip writer John Aubrey that he had been a 'schoolmaster in the country', however, is rather more pertinent. There have been numerous dramatists whose day job was teaching, and the job of master in a school run along sixteenth-century humanist principles would have been a particularly helpful first career move. Teaching Latin would have enabled him to consolidate his own knowledge of the standard school texts, from Julius Caesar's histories of the wars and politics of Rome, to the poetry of transformation and myth in Ovid's *Metamorphoses*. And his lack of a university degree would not be unusual for an assistant master.

The curriculum for Stratford grammar school from the period is no longer extant, but from the surviving curricula of other schools we can presume that as a pupil, and perhaps later as a teacher, Shakespeare would have engaged in the practice of double translation, first from Latin into English and then back into as accurate an imitation of the original Latin as possible. Imitation, however, can also be creative; the great humanist scholar Erasmus advocated in *A Method of Study* that boys should also be allowed to play games with the texts they read, noting that the great stories of classical myth are found in different forms, and that it might therefore be both instructive and entertaining for boys to be allowed to write variations on a given story.

Play performance, both in Latin and English, was a valued recreational activity in many schools when Shakespeare was young. Besides being fun, it trained boys in public speaking and developed their memories. A number of the plays or interludes that still survive from the mid-sixteenth century were written by the schoolmasters of the London choir schools, the Chapel Royal and St Paul's, whose children also performed plays regularly at court, and some were published probably because printers expected to be able to sell copies to grammar schools up and down the land. As a schoolmaster himself, Shakespeare would have had the opportunity to write his own plays and direct his charges in them. It would have been an invaluable education for an aspiring dramatist. There is no proof of this, but it would explain how the boy from Stratford acquired the necessary literary and theatrical knowledge, and the opportunity to practice his writing. But it too does not explain how he made the transition to a professional theatrical career.

Shakespeare the actor

Of the many possibilities that have been suggested, there are two that are worth considering, the first of which is also connected to being a schoolmaster. In this scenario, with the help of John Cottom, the master of Stratford grammar school, he secured a job as a teacher in the Catholic household of Alexander Hoghton of Lea in Lancashire. Cottom came from nearby Tarnacre, and was the brother of a recusant Catholic priest, who would shortly be executed. Hoghton's will, drawn up and proved in 1581, bequeaths his musical instruments and set of play clothes to his brother or, if he has no use for these, to his neighbour, Sir Thomas Hesketh, adding that he wishes Hesketh to be 'friendly unto Fulke Gillom and William Shakeshafte, now dwelling with me'. Hesketh had close ties with Lord Strange, and if this Shakeshafte is Shakespeare, it might have given him the necessary contacts for a route into Strange's company of actors in the early 1580s. But it is by no means certain. Shakeshafte was a fairly common name in Lancashire.

An alternative suggestion is that Shakespeare joined one of the numerous playing companies that passed through Stratford in the 1580s. One colourful suggestion is that he was taken up by the Queen's Men when they visited Stratford in 1586–7; they were a man short because one actor, William Knell, had been killed in a street brawl in Thame in Oxfordshire. Did Shakespeare fill his place when they got to Stratford and leave on the road with them? Within the year, Knell's widow, Rebecca, married John Hemmings (or Heminges), another actor in the company, who would become Shakespeare's friend, executor, and one of the two actors responsible for the publication of his collected plays.

In the wording of the 1572 Act for the Punishment of Vagabonds, all 'fencers, bearwards, common players in interludes, minstrels, jugglers, pedlars, tinkers and petty chapmen' had to have an aristocratic patron, or a licence from two justices of the peace in order to protect them from the charge of vagrancy as 'rogues, vagabonds and sturdy beggars'. This system of patronage was mutually beneficial: the actors could travel and earn their living; their patrons enjoyed the kudos from having their servants advertise their name and prestige, and might also have the opportunity to bring them to court to entertain the queen.

The Queen's Men came into being ten years after this act was passed, taking the best players from other acting companies to form a pre-eminent troop. A number were drawn from the company belonging to the Earl of Leicester – Elizabeth's favourite – presumably with his great good will, and even connivance at the honour. Since Thomas Walsingham, the queen's spymaster, took a surprisingly active interest in the company's formation, it is possible that one ulterior motive was that it served the purpose of showing an aspect of the queen to her people in parts of the country to which she would never go in person. Conversely, while on their travels, they might also supply intelligence back to the court on political activity in the country.

The Queen's Men's repertoire was often rambunctious. Led by Richard Tarlton, the famous clown, loved and admired for his extemporising wit, they incorporated a physical style of performance, and stock comedy routines; printed versions of their playtexts may therefore not do them justice. They were also politically correct, as befitted their name and patron; their version of a King John play, *The Troublesome Reign of King John* (printed in 1591), is very much more overtly Protestant and partisan than Shakespeare's version of the same story. There are other tantalising connections with Shakespeare's work: their repertoire included a King Lear play, and *The Taming of a Shrew* (a play with a story similar to Shakespeare's *The Taming of the Shrew*, but set in Athens). Clearly they went down well in the country as they continued to tour, even as far as Scotland and the north of Ireland. But there are no records of them performing at court between Christmas 1591 and their final performance there on Twelfth Night 1594.

Whether or not Shakespeare was in Lancashire in his teens, or started his career with the Queen's Men, a period connected in some way with Strange's Men some time in the late 1580s and early 1590s is the most likely preparation for his later success. He is not mentioned in any surviving list of their players, but it is this company that supplies eight of the ten actors who in 1594 would form the new Chamberlain's company. The first unequivocal mention of Shakespeare in theatrical records is at Easter the following year when he is named along with the actors William Kemp and Richard Burbage as one of the payees for two performances at court by the Lord Chamberlain's Men during the intervening Christmas season, for which they earned a total of £20.

Shakespeare the poet

The London theatres were closed for much of 1593–4 because of the plague, and the acting companies were forced on the road. Shakespeare, however, may have gone back to Stratford. The result, wherever he was, was two long narrative poems about love: *Venus and Adonis* and *The Rape of Lucrece*. These two poems also show him recruiting a patron, Henry Wriothesley, Earl of Southampton. *Venus and Adonis* does not bear Shakespeare's name on the title page but it includes a signed dedicatory letter from Shakespeare to Southampton, in which he wonders 'how I shall offend in dedicating my unpolished lines to your Lordship'. He promises 'graver labour' in the future – if Southampton will allow it. The poem was printed and published in 1593 initially by Richard Field, also from Stratford and three years Shakespeare's senior; it is very carefully produced. It was immensely popular and there were fifteen further editions before 1640, although few copies survive, which suggests that the books were read until they disintegrated. The dedication to Southampton in *The Rape of Lucrece* the following year is more confident, and suggests that Southampton had reciprocated: 'The warrant I have of your honourable disposition, not the worth of my untutored lines, makes it assured of acceptance. What I have done is yours, what I have to do is yours, being part in all I have, devoted yours.'

The sonnets were not published until 1609, but some at least were written rather earlier. Numbers 138 and 144 appear in *The Passionate Pilgrim* (1599), a collection of short poems by a variety of authors including a version of Marlowe's 'Come live with me and be my love'. Other poems in that collection seem to echo both that and Shakespeare's *Venus and Adonis*. In 1598 Francis Meres, in a book called *Palladis Tamia* or 'Treasury of the Arts and Sciences', had noted that the sonnets were circulating 'amongst his friends' in manuscript. He describes them as 'sugared', and Shakespeare himself as honey-tongued – epithets quoted endlessly by later scholars. Meres's similar comments on a number of other English writers, some of whom we no longer rate very highly, have suggested to modern critics that he was not very discriminating. But that is to miss the point. Honey-tongued in this context means the bee-like practice of sucking the sweetness from the 'flowers' or best examples of the ancients, and also the ability to cull witty and improving sentiments from rather sourer subject matter. Throughout this long book, Meres's purpose is to demonstrate that there is a modern English counterpart for every achievement of the Greeks and Romans in every field of human endeavour, and that English writers are every bit as good as the ancients in every genre and form. The book itself is in fact a virtual copy of a classical precedent with the names changed. If he discriminates it is because he mentions some modern poets once only, whereas Shakespeare is listed repeatedly.

Appreciation of the poems has been sidetracked by the desire to make them tell a story about his life: what exactly was his relationship with Southampton? Who are the young man and the dark lady referred to in the sonnets? Was Shakespeare homosexual? That word did not exist in his period, and definition of the *idea* in historical terms is therefore fraught with difficulty. But Shakespeare's skill as a poet, in both his dramatic and non-dramatic works, is to allow a wealth of possible meanings to flourish in his wordplay, and individuals of all genders and sexual orientations can now find in his sonnets the words to express personal feelings of love. Rather than attempting to pin down these jewel-like creations as code for some unverifiable biography, we could have more fun with them if we joined in with the rhetorical games he plays in them. We might also rekindle interest in the narrative poems, which have been largely neglected in recent criticism.

Shakespeare, gentleman

In 1596 Shakespeare obtained a coat of arms, not for himself but for his father. John himself had applied some twenty years earlier, but had been turned down. On this occasion the application was successful (although not without some later misgivings about granting honours to mere players). The grounds given for the grant were that John had been a justice of the peace and a Queen's Bailiff, and had married 'an heir of Arden'; the Arden family were substantial landholders in Warwickshire. Biographers have speculated on William's motives, and modern egalitarianism has been a little embarrassed by this apparent social climbing. But in an age when the circles in which you moved, what people thought about you, and even how you were allowed to dress were determined by social rank, one might sympathise.

In *King John* the character most suited to inherit the kingdom is the one disqualified by birth: the Bastard, whose satirical running commentary leaves us in no doubt of the incompetence of those in power. In *The Winter's Tale*, the Clown, the Old Shepherd's son, swaggers in his newfound gentlemanly status at the end of the play and boasts, comically, that he is a 'gentleman born before my father' – just like William himself. The Old Shepherd, who has behaved with good sense, rectitude, honour, and gentleness throughout, reminds him 'we must be gentle, now we are gentlemen' (5.2.126–47). Did Shakespeare too think it ridiculous that under a system of inherited social status, honour increases with distance from the act that occasioned the elevation? Who knows, but I like to think so.

Shakespeare, the King's Man

Almost immediately on coming to the English throne in 1603, James I took all the London playing companies into the patronage of members of the royal family. He probably did this in an attempt to exercise more control over them, but the arrangement was also financially beneficial, at least for Shakespeare's company. Thus, the Chamberlain's Men became the King's Men, or more formally, His Majesties Servants. Their main rivals in London, the Admiral's Men, were taken into the service of the queen. Shakespeare and his fellow sharers (those who had a share in the ownership of the company) were now Grooms of the Chamber, each entitled to a grant of red livery to mark James's coronation. Between this date and Shakespeare's death in 1616, the company was paid for at least one hundred and seven appearances at court, far more than in Elizabeth's reign.

Throughout Shakespeare's working life, one of the reasons given by the Privy Council to the City of London as to why acting companies should be allowed to mount public performances in London was that it provided the necessary rehearsal before a performance at court. More importantly perhaps, it enabled theatre companies to be self-financing so that the court did not need to bear all of the rehearsal and production costs of a single night's entertainment. Now, when the public theatres were closed for many months during 1609–11 because of plague, the accounts, which record expenditure on entertainment for the Royal household, show that for two Christmases running, Shakespeare's company had been given a special payment for rehearsals as well as for the performance itself:

> John Hemmings ... for himself and the rest of his company
> being restrained from public playing within the city of London
> in the time of infection during the space of six weeks in which
> time they practised privately for his majesty's service. £30

This means that plays like *Cymbeline* and *The Winter's Tale* may well have had their first performances at court. Certain similarities between these two plays and the court masques and other spectacular court entertainments known to have been performed in the winters of 1609–10 and 1610–11 respectively suggest that they may even have been commissioned to fit a prescribed theme.

In *Cymbeline*, for example, the Celtic British princess Imogen travels to Milford Haven in Wales to find her banished husband who is returning as part of an invading Roman army. Once in Wales, she meets her long lost brothers who return from hunting to find her in their cave in a drugged sleep, apparently dead. It was probably performed at court during the same Christmas season as a 'barriers' (or courtly, martial exercise), in which James I's eldest son, Prince Henry – in the role of Meliades, knight of God, and heir to the Celtic Arthurian values – took on challengers in a feat of arms. A scene in the short play written by Ben Jonson to introduce the event showed a young woman, representing honour and chivalry, asleep as if dead in a cave in Wales, waiting for Henry/Meliades to reawaken her. June 1610 would see the investiture of Henry as Prince of Wales. The investiture itself would be marked by a masque commissioned by his mother, Queen Anne, in which court ladies danced, dressed as nymphs representing the rivers of England and Wales, who have also gathered at Milford Haven. This great natural port had huge significance for the royal family. James's great grandfather, Henry Richmond, had landed there on his return to the country before vanquishing Richard III at the battle of Bosworth, and thereby becoming Henry VII.

The Winter's Tale too is about the restitution of a royal family. In this play, King Leontes accuses his wife Hermione of adultery and orders the abandonment of their baby daughter. Although time jumps forwards by sixteen years in the middle of the play to allow the baby to grow to womanhood, the progress of the seasons appears to work steadily backwards from winter, via a midsummer sheep-shearing, to the return of spring when the princess is found. In one of its most celebrated scenes, Hermione, long thought to be dead, appears as a statue, which is then brought to life. This play may well have been performed at court in the same season as Jonson's masques *Love Freed from Ignorance and Folly* and *Love Restored*, which share its theme of love imprisoned in a cold climate, and celebrate James's manipulation of time in the creation of a realm where it is perpetual spring. It also seems to have inspired a succession of court masques written to celebrate the marriage of James's daughter Elizabeth, all featuring moving statues. Elizabeth and her husband would later briefly become King and Queen of Bohemia, before being removed by a rebellion, which instigated the beginning of the Thirty Years' War. Their short reign earned them the soubriquets of Winter King and Queen. This unexpected topicality perhaps accounts for the play's continuing popularity at the Stuart court; it enjoyed at least six performances there over twenty years.

Unlike the masques, however, the multi-faceted structure of Shakespeare's plays means that they are not confined to a specific occasion. Far from being eulogies to the king, they examine royal injustice. Both *Cymbeline* and *The Winter's Tale* were seen in public performances at the Globe and, along with *Macbeth*, were described by the astrologer Simon Forman in 1612 – three of a mere handful of surviving descriptions of Shakespeare's plays in performance during his lifetime.

Shakespeare, the portraits

Portraits of Shakespeare are equally thin on the ground. The best known is probably the engraving by Martin Droeshout the younger that forms the frontispiece to the Folio of 1623, the first collected works of Shakespeare. Martin was the third in a line of Flemish engravers living in London, but only twenty-two when the Folio was published. There are some things not quite right about this image. The forehead looks excessively high, even for one who was bald on top, and the head, which is out of proportion with the body, does not seem to sit naturally on the neck, which seems impossibly long. The sitter has bulging eyes, which has added to speculation about the cause of Shakespeare's comparatively early death.

There are a number of other portraits supposedly of Shakespeare, of which the most convincing is the Chandos. It was one of the first bequests to the National Portrait Gallery in London, but at the end of the seventeenth century was almost certainly in the possession of the actor Thomas Betterton. This rather more physiologically convincing image shows a serious and thoughtful-looking man with a receding hairline and prominent forehead. He wears a plain dark doublet with a simple lawn collar, its strings undone, and sports a gold earring. The dress is sober and unostentatious, but both the earring and the slight *déshabillé* denote 'poet', as they do in the famous portrait of John Donne.

A recent subject of intense speculation has been the Cobbe portrait. This shows a very richly dressed, aristocratic-looking man in a rich black doublet embroidered with gold, and a fine standing lace collar in the court fashion of *c.* 1610. It is one of a number of nearly identical copies of the same image. Despite his success at court by this date, it is unlikely that someone of Shakespeare's standing would have thought it prudent to sit for a portrait dressed as an aristocrat. The self-portrait of star actor and wealthy gentleman Richard Burbage in the Dulwich Picture Gallery, for instance, shows a man quite soberly dressed. It is also unlikely that so many copies of this image should have been made before Shakespeare achieved pre-eminent status as the nation's poet. The sitter was probably Sir Thomas Overbury, a court favourite who had achieved a certain notoriety at that time, and was shortly to die in suspicious circumstances.

There are similar doubts about the Grafton portrait. This shows a fashionably dressed young man with a painted label announcing that the sitter was aged twenty-four in 1588. He is the right age, but that is all. His slashed red doublet and fine lawn collar bears great similarity in style of dress and presentation to the portrait discovered on a builder's rubbish dump when work was being done on Corpus Christi College Cambridge in 1953, which was subsequently claimed to be a picture of Christopher Marlowe. Both ascriptions are equally dubious, although attractive to many because the sitters correspond to a certain notion of what a poet *should* look like: slim, elegant, and refined, like Joseph Fiennes in *Shakespeare in Love*.

The profession of writer, of course, is not conducive to maintaining such a body shape. Long hours sitting at the desk, possibly into the small hours when everyone else has gone to bed and the house is quiet, makes for a certain jowly puffiness. The image that is rarely reproduced as a likeness of the poet is the monument near Shakespeare's grave in Stratford parish church, famously described by the critic John Dover Wilson as looking like a 'pork butcher'. This style of funeral monument was, however, fashionable in the early seventeenth century. It has suffered over the years from remodelling and repainting, but shows a balding, rather stout man, looking confidently out into the world – as well he might.

The Stratford register records that William Shakespeare, 'Gent', was buried on 25 April 1616. Unsurprisingly, popular tradition gives his death day, like his birthday, as 23 April, St George's day. He was barely fifty-two.

Shakespeare's theatres

Sixteenth-century London was dotted with places in which plays were performed. Playing took place at court, in private houses, in inns, and in the Inns of Court, in schools, and, most visibly to all, in the streets and on the Thames, with spectacular processions and displays to mark coronations, investitures, weddings, funerals, and a range of other events both civic and royal. The first purpose-built theatre in England, however, was erected by the carpenter and architect James Burbage in 1576 on a piece of land just outside the jurisdiction of the City of London in Shoreditch. It was called the Theatre, from the Greek *theatron*, which means 'viewing place'. It was circular, with tiers of galleries surrounding a yard open to the sky. James was also a player in the service of the Earl of Leicester. The Theatre was initially home to Leicester's Men and later saw performances by all the leading companies of the day. James was an irascible figure, forever arguing with the authorities (who neglected no opportunity in trying to close him down, although they did not succeed) and, on at least one occasion, even falling out with his own son, Richard, the leading actor with the Chamberlain's Men, Shakespeare's company from 1594 onwards.

The Theatre was followed in 1587 by the Rose, built in the Liberty of the Clink on Bankside, the south bank of the Thames, by businessman, pawnbroker, and theatrical impresario Philip Henslowe. Close to the City, but again outside its juris-diction, the area attracted a range of recreational businesses, including bull and bear baiting, and brothels. Amongst its gardens, orchards, and fishmongers' holding ponds, stocked with carp and pike, which made use of the marshy ground, were also some rather smelly industries such as a soap works, tanning and dye-works, perhaps a terracotta factory, and later a brewery.

The Rose must have been a success, for within five years Henslowe was enlarging it. Excavations of the site have shown that he pushed the walls out into an odd-shaped pocket of land at the back, making the building more of a horse-shoe than a circle. More importantly, they revealed the foundations for two stages, both with angled sides. The earlier was very shallow; the second, larger and rather more thrust out, allowing spectators to gather round it.

The only contemporary illustration of the interior of an Elizabethan theatre is the famous 'De Witt' drawing of the Swan, built in 1595 on Bankside by Francis Langley. But this drawing raises many more questions than it answers. The Dutchman Johannes De Witt probably visited the year after the theatre opened and included a drawing of the building in a letter to his friend Aernout van Buchel. The original is lost, but van Buchel copied it into his journal – we cannot tell how accurately.

The drawing may show several different points in time simultaneously. A trumpeter in the turret at the top of the tiring house that formed the rear of the stage is probably signalling that a performance is about to begin. But on stage, three actors perform an unidentified play, with two female characters, one seated and one standing, and what appears to be a comic or caricature male character with a pointed beard and a staff, making an exaggerated bow. There are figures in the gallery over the stage, though it is impossible to tell whether these are visitors, or other actors and musicians. The galleries and yard are empty, probably because De Witt (or van Buchel) was not interested in drawing the audience, but perhaps because De Witt was present at a rehearsal. There are pillars positioned in the centre back of the stage supporting a small roof, while some structures visible underneath the stage may be trestles. The Swan was a multi-purpose building, sometimes used for fencing displays and competitions. It is therefore possible that the section of stage not covered by the roof was removable for such events, allowing the roofed stage area to be occupied by the judges.

Just as significant, though less often reproduced, is the letter in Latin that accompanies the picture. From this it is clear that De Witt's interest, as a foreign tourist and humanist scholar, is the extent to which London's buildings imitate classical style. He describes St Paul's cathedral as like a temple to the goddess Diana; and he lists five beautiful 'amphitheatres' – the Rose, the Swan, and the two theatres to the north of the city (i.e. the Theatre and Curtain), plus an animal baiting arena. The Swan, he says, held three thousand spectators, and the wooden pillars supporting the stage roof are so skilfully painted that even the most curious and discerning or nosy (*nasutissimos*) of observers might think they were marble.

In the winter of 1598–9, the Burbages dismantled the Theatre because of a dispute with the owner of the land on which it was built. The timbers were taken to the yard of the carpenter Peter Street, where they were reused to create the frame for a new theatre building. A few months later this was transported across the river to a building plot which they had secured at a low rent near the Rose on Bankside, and became the Globe. James Burbage had died and his sons Cuthbert and Richard raised extra funds for this rebuild by selling shares in the building to Shakespeare, Hemmings, and a small group of other actor-sharers in the company, who were then also made joint lessees of the land on which it stood. Although they were reusing the old timbers, it seems likely that they took the opportunity to make a larger, more impressive building, for immediately after it opened, Henslowe, not to be outdone, commissioned Street to build him a new theatre, the Fortune. This was to be exactly 'according to the manner and fashion' of the Globe – but square. One thing is clear: there was no such thing as 'the' Elizabethan theatre; all theatres were different.

JIGS AND A TALE OF BAWDRY

An afternoon at the theatre commonly ended in a dance or jig. A handful of these survive in manuscript and show a combination of raucous song, defamatory dialogue, and dance. Shakespeare's company may have modified this practice, for Thomas Platter, visiting from abroad writes:

> At the end of the comedy they danced according to their custom with extreme elegance. Two in men's clothes and two in women's gave this performance, in wonderful combination with each other.

In the absence of any hard archaeological or documentary evidence about the size and design of the Globe itself, scholars advising on the building of the replica Globe in London (which opened in 1997) pored over the Fortune contract for details of the dimensions of that building. Possibly the most significant require-ment in that contract is that the stage, 'like unto the stage of ... the Globe', should be forty-three feet wide, extend to the middle of the yard, and be covered by a tile roof. This is a very wide, and a very deep stage, much larger than either of the stages at the Rose. Unfortunately, the contract refers to a plan that has not survived, and we do not know its shape, whether square or angled.

Playing outside, particularly in winter, has its drawbacks and it was the Burbages' long-term ambition to open an indoor theatre. The greater comfort (and of course the greater expense in having to light the stage and auditorium with candles) would mean higher ticket prices and a different clientele. In 1596, James Burbage had obtained a lease on the refectory building of the former Dominican or 'Blackfriars' monastery on the north back of the Thames. Because of its monastic past, this area too was a liberty, outside the jurisdiction of the City of London. But the residents of the complex, including the company's patron, Lord Hunsdon, and Richard Field, first printer of Shakespeare's poems, were anxious about the possibility of disorder from crowds visiting a public theatre. Their petition to the Privy Council resulted in permission being denied. Richard Burbage therefore let the building to a boys' company, who, at sixpence for the cheapest seats, charged much higher prices than did the public theatre adult companies. This company was probably acceptable to the residents because of the fiction that they were allowing a high class audience to witness rehearsals of plays prior to performances at court. Meanwhile Burbage continued to acquire neighbouring properties. With a decline in the fortunes of the boys' company, Burbage bought back the lease, then reassigned it to include Shakespeare, Hemmings, Condell, and three other King's Men sharers as lessees; their company commenced playing in the theatre in 1609.

The argument that use of the Blackfriars building influenced Shakespeare's writing for the theatre in his late plays is overdone. The rectangular hall, supplied with a stage at one end and with galleries built against the walls for the audience, would have been very like the playing spaces that the players had always encountered when they performed in halls at court, in the Inns of Court, in great houses, or in civic buildings.

Shakespeare in print

In their hard covers on library bookshelves, the complete works of Shakespeare may look authoritative and tangible, but they are every bit as difficult to pin down as his life story. Apart from four pages of the manuscript play of *Sir Thomas More*, which are generally thought to be in Shakespeare's handwriting, there are no surviving autograph manuscripts of his plays or poems. Thus, and with only a small handful of very brief descriptions of the plays in performance in his lifetime, almost all our evidence for his work comes from printed texts.

Shakespeare is traditionally credited with writing thirty-seven plays, all but one of which (*Pericles*) appeared in the so-called 'First Folio' collection of his dramatic works in 1623, seven years after his death. Without this book, many of the plays for which he is now most famous – *Twelfth Night*, *Antony and Cleopatra*, and *Macbeth*, for instance – would be unknown. It is likely, however, that *Pericles* and a few of the earliest and latest plays in the Folio (*Titus Andronicus*, *1 Henry VI*, and *Henry VIII*, for instance) may have been written in some form of collaboration with other writers. In addition to *Sir Thomas More*, there are a few other plays not included in the Folio in which Shakespeare may have had a hand, such as *Arden of Faversham*, *Edward III*, *Two Noble Kinsmen*, and *Double Falsehood*.

Sixteen of the Folio play titles (including *Pericles* and most of the history plays) were also printed as single plays in smaller and therefore cheaper quarto (and occasionally octavo) format during his lifetime. The problem is that there are significant differences between many of these texts and the same plays as printed in the Folio. Are these differences the result of careless printing, or corrupt practices, or playhouse revisions, or Shakespeare changing his mind, or a combination of two or more of these activities? And how might we tell? These are important questions since such differences alter a play's meaning and dramatic effect.

FOLIOS, QUARTOS, AND OCTAVOS

The terms 'folio', 'quarto', and 'octavo' refer to the results when paper is folded in different ways to construct a book.

Folio

A sheet of paper, folded once, produces two leaves (folios). In order to facilitate the stitching of these folded sheets together, and to produce a book of uniform thickness, a folio book is made up of multiple 'gatherings' or 'quires', each consisting of three or four sheets of paper folded together. The Shakespeare First Folio is a 'folio in sixes', that is, gatherings of three sheets of paper, folded together to make six leaves (twelve pages). The outer sheet in the gathering therefore contains the first and the twelfth pages of the gathering on one side of the paper and the second and eleventh pages on the other.

Quarto

A quarto book is made by folding a single sheet of paper twice, thereby producing a gathering of four leaves. The first, fourth, fifth, and eighth pages in each gathering are printed on one side of the paper and the second, third, sixth, and seventh pages on the other.

Octavo

An octavo book is made by folding a single sheet of paper three times, producing a gathering of eight leaves.

Shakespeare: the 1623 Folio

A folio is a large book, expensive to make and therefore to buy since its preparation, printing, and marketing ties up a considerable amount of resources: printing presses, workmen's hours, type, and paper. Folios were therefore customarily reserved for serious subjects (e.g. sermons, bibles, legal tomes). Ben Jonson was the first person to publish plays and masques in folio format in the collected edition of his works in 1616 – the year Shakespeare died.

Shakespeare's collected plays were published by his friends and fellow actors, John Hemmings and Henry Condell. He had left both of them money in his will to buy mourning rings. Perhaps he hoped, or had asked, that they would arrange this publication. The humorous pleading of the opening of their address to the book's potential readers that they buy the book before giving an opinion on it is a necessary attempt to recoup the considerable expenditure involved in printing it, but it has such a ring of honesty that I like to think they genuinely saw the project as a labour of love toward their friend and colleague:

> From the most able, to him that can but spell: there you are numbered. We had rather you were weighed. Especially, when the fate of all books depends upon your capacities: and not of your heads alone, but of your purses. Well, it is now public, and you will stand for your privileges we know, to read, and censure. Do so, but buy it first. ... Judge your sixe-pen'orth, your shilling's worth, your five shillings' worth at a time, or higher, so you rise to the just rates, and welcome. But whatever you do, buy.
>
> (Preface, To the great Variety of Readers, *Mr William Shakespeare's Comedies Histories and Tragedies*, 1623)

In 1623 a bound copy of this book might typically cost £1 (the equivalent of three or four weeks' work for a skilled artisan).

Some 228 copies still survive, which means that it is not particularly rare. Many copies are in institutional libraries, however, and there is considerable excitement when one comes to market. In this century, copies have so far sold for between £2.5 million and £3.7 million.

The printing and copying process

The 'allowed' copy of a play, that is, the manuscript which had been licensed for performance by the Master of the Revels and which served as the prompt book, was a valuable commodity. It could, for example, be shown to the dignitaries of towns in which the actors wished to play, in order to reinforce their credentials and gain permission to perform. Since the process of printing tends to destroy manuscripts, which get broken up and divided between different compositors or typesetters in order to speed the process, this would not have been the copy sent to the printer; some other version of the play would need to be found, or the prompt book would have to be copied by a scribe.

Every time something is copied, change is inevitable. Sometimes, the copyist might attempt a conscious improvement. Walter Crane, the scribe thought to be responsible for copying the manuscripts from which a number of the plays in the Folio were printed, is noted for his introduction of heavier, more 'literary' punctuation, and for peppering the text with what have been termed 'swibs' (single words in brackets). Sometimes, however, these changes will be accidental: the person doing the copying, whether author, scribe, or printer, makes a mistake. In addition, since spelling was not fixed at this time, and different people had different spelling preferences, the copyist will inevitably introduce inadvertent spelling changes, even if he is trying to copy exactly.

The sixteenth- or seventeenth-century print worker was paid piece-work, that is, according to the amount he produced each day. The compositor (the type-setter) and press-man (the man who operated the printing press) would be allocated a certain amount of text to be printed on a certain number of sheets of paper. But unexpected difficulties always arise when setting from manuscript copy. Handwriting, even by the same person in the same manuscript, can vary in size and clarity depending on the speed at which it was written; crossings out and insertions can make handwriting difficult to read and also make it difficult to gauge how much space the text will take up in print. Pragmatic decisions on the part of the compositor that affect the nature and arrangement of the words on the page are therefore inevitable. Thus we regularly find instances where compositors have had to lose space by setting prose as verse, or to gain it by setting verse as prose, perhaps in some desperate circumstances, excising whole passages.

Given the nature of the technology and the pressure of work in the print shop, proof-reading tended to be haphazard. Only a few pages of text would be in type on any given day, before the blocks of type were taken apart and redistributed so that the type-setting and printing process could continue. It would therefore have required daily attendance at the print shop for an author to be able to proof-read his own work. Those operating the presses would only scan the first impression for the detection of obvious blunders. Although the master printer might inspect his men's work by reading through a printed sheet, he would usually not be able to check the fidelity of printed text to the copy, even if he had thought it necessary. As a result, he might request a change where in fact no error existed, or alternatively correct an actual error by introducing a different one. Since printing would not cease for this proof 'correction' process, the final pile of printed sheets might include both corrected and uncorrected copies, all of which would be used in making up the finished books.

While most Elizabethan printers tried to do a professional job, these practical difficulties mean that no two editions of any book printed at this period will be identical even if one is directly set up from the other, and there may well be variants in different copies even from the same edition. For example it is thought that the First Quarto of *The Merchant of Venice* was used as the copy text for the Second Quarto. Comparing the two, D.F. McKenzie found approximately 3,200 variant readings, mostly minor spelling and punctuation changes, but including some attempts at substantive correction.

Revisions

Sometimes, those responsible for holding or copying manuscripts would make more conscious changes to a text. The 1606 Act to Restrain Abuses of Players, for instance, forbade the use of the word 'God', or oaths such as 'Swounds' (God's wounds). Plays printed after the introduction of this act therefore substitute with other more innocuous words such as 'heaven'.

But much more interesting is that sometimes the differences between quarto and folio versions of a Shakespeare play amount to radical revision, even wholesale rewriting, creating two or more versions of a play with very different potential for meaning. Sometimes, the quality of this revision suggests that it may have been done by Shakespeare himself. Sometimes, plays may have been cut or revised by the theatre companies. Sometimes, hired actors with no financial stake in the company sought to make a little extra money by writing out what they could remember from performing in a play, sometimes incorporating quotations from other plays, filling in the gaps with their own new material, and selling the result to a printer. Inevitably, critics sometimes disagree as to which is which. But since the reason for reading and watching Shakespeare is the value and meaning we can derive from his work now, and since meaning and value alter when the text alters, it is important even for 'beginners' to be aware of what the problems are when we use the seemingly self-evident phrase 'the works of Shakespeare'.

Recently some scholars have advanced the argument that writers commonly wrote more than might be performed on the stage in the time available. There are two unknowns associated with this argument. The first is whether the 'two hours traffic of the stage' described by the Prologue to *Romeo and Juliet* is a timespan to be taken absolutely literally, or whether it means anything under three hours by the church clock, or by the pocket sun-dial that a wealthier patron might carry. Play performances in the public theatres began at 2pm and civic authorities wanted to prevent audience members thronging the streets after dark, which would be as early as 4pm in winter. Actors, of course, were not noted for their obedience to orders from that quarter. The second unknown is the speed at which actors delivered their lines. It is my experience that Shakespeare is easier to comprehend when spoken relatively quickly – making it simpler to grasp the overall shape of a long sentence.

It is true that on a few occasions both Ben Jonson and John Webster complained that actors cut their work for performance and announced that they were taking the opportunity of print to put the record straight. But Shakespeare, as an actor himself, may have taken a more theatrically driven approach to his writing, and as the resident dramatist and company sharer, he was better placed to retain control over what was played.

Editorial practice

When a play exists in two variant versions both of which, judging by the quality of the verse, seem to be reliably by Shakespeare, editors and performers are faced with a problem: what should be understood, printed, and performed as '*the* play'? There are, for instance, two very different versions of *King Lear*, a Quarto (1608) and the Folio, both of which contain extended passages which are not in the other, as well as thousands of other minor variants, and which present contradictory versions of the conduct of the war in the play. There are three early versions of *Hamlet*: two reliably by Shakespeare (the Second Quarto of 1604–5 and the Folio), as well as one (the First Quarto of 1603) that seems to have been put together by actors. Although we can never say what Shakespeare *intended* to write, we can, and I think we should, try to disentangle the early multiple versions of important plays such as these and distinguish between the different ethos of each version. What is it that one version allows us to think, feel, and understand, which the other version perhaps does not? And why?

Earlier editors assumed that all early printed texts were faulty, and saw it as their task to reconstruct Shakespeare's lost original. The usual editorial practice was to conflate: that is, to base an edition on one particular version but to add in all the 'missing' passages from the other, and to correct it where it was thought to be inaccurate. Where two reliable texts were broadly in agreement, but still contained variant readings, they would usually choose the more 'difficult' or ambiguous, on the grounds that a compositor, or other copyist who was not the author, would have tended to simplify words or phrases that he did not understand.

Conflated versions can be very long. Peter Hall's 'uncut' *Hamlet* with Albert Finney in 1976 ran to four and a quarter hours. But after the publication of the Oxford *Complete Works of*

Shakespeare (edited by Stanley Wells and Gary Taylor) in 1986, which printed editions of both the Quarto and Folio versions of *King Lear*, editors realised that by conflating these early texts they were creating a play that had never existed before. Where space and publisher finances allow, they now prefer to supply the reader with parallel texts.

It is the job of an editor to present readers with all the evidence, whether in footnotes or parallel text editions, but actors can only play one thing at a time. Theatre directors therefore have to make choices between variant readings. In addition, they inevitably want to make their own mark with a production, and might try to do that by cutting or rearranging a text to fit a particular 'concept'. They may also feel they need to cut the text in order to make space for the use of theatre technology, scene changes, and effects, all of which take time to stage. The net result is that each new prompt book and performance presents a different version of the text.

The Holy Grail in Shakespeare studies and performance would be a complete manuscript of a major play in his handwriting. In the absence of such an artefact, we need to look behind the printed surfaces of the surviving playbooks to try to discern how they came into being and judge what kind of manuscript was used as the copytext.

The basic principle of forensic science is that every contact leaves a trace. This is also true of printed books. Printed texts that include stray notes on properties or actors' names probably derive ultimately from a manuscript in use in the theatre, while those that are vague about the number of characters on stage or are inconsistent in their use of speech prefixes might suggest an author at work on a pre-rehearsal version. Editors and critics look for these idiosyncrasies as clues to the nature of the manuscript behind the printed text, and therefore to the status of that text.

THE MANUSCRIPTS BEHIND THE PRINTED TEXTS

There may be as many as five or more distinct classes of ultimate manuscript copy for the printed texts of Shakespeare, always recognising that in individual cases, a further manuscript – a scribal transcript – may intervene between any one of these and the printed version:

1 Authorial draft

A draft of the play written before the necessary process of revision for theatrical performance. Texts printed from such copy might occasionally show indecision about the names of characters, or the characters needed on stage in a particular scene. The conventional technical term for this type of manuscript is 'foul papers' but this has unfortunate overtones of immorality or lack of hygiene and is misleading. The 1604 Quarto of *Hamlet* and the Folio version of *Richard III*, and perhaps *Timon of Athens*, are examples.

2 Authorial revision

A text revised by the author for performance. It is now widely (but not universally) accepted that the Folio versions of *King Lear* and *Hamlet* fall into this category.

3 Actors' reconstruction

A company may occasionally and unexpectedly be called upon to perform a text for which it does not have access to its own original prompt book, perhaps because it is on tour. The actors may then be compelled to reconstruct the prompt book by collectively dictating their parts. Such a text might provide valuable evidence for the overall structure and shape of the play as performed, but individual words and phrases would be subject to the vagaries of individual actors' memories. It seems possible that the Quarto text of *Richard III* is the result of such a process.

THE MANUSCRIPTS BEHIND THE
PRINTED TEXTS (*cont.*)

4 Management version

We know that Philip Henslowe, owner of the Rose Theatre, sometimes sought to breathe new life into an existing play by employing another writer to revise the text or add further attractions. I remain unconvinced that any Shakespeare texts are printed from manuscripts in this category, although Wells and Taylor, without inventing a new term, have suggested that *Measure for Measure* and *Macbeth* – both of which they claim to contain revisions by Middleton – might fall into it. A modern counterpart would be the published screenplay of, for example, Kenneth Branagh's *Henry V*. It was common practice in the eighteenth and nineteenth centuries to publish the text of Shakespeare 'as performed' in the theatre. There are a large number of such publications deriving from productions of Shakespeare at Covent Garden by John Philip Kemble. This practice is also not uncommon in the modern theatre with productions of new or less familiar works, where the souvenir programme is also the text of the play. But in all such cases, the book may well have been printed before final decisions about the performance text have been worked out in rehearsal; despite their claims, such texts are not necessarily exactly the text of the play as performed.

5 Derivative version

A version of a play or its subject matter, recreated by one or more individuals without access to any existing full text, who wish to capitalise on the success of the original, or that of its author. Such versions are commonly called 'memorial reconstructions' although that term is not particularly helpful, since the object is not necessarily to reconstruct the play as played, and the means whereby it is done may not be memorial. The authors might, for example, want to improve the play, correcting perceived faults in the structure or meaning, perhaps strengthening a particular political or religious line. Re-creation might be achieved through a variety of

THE MANUSCRIPTS BEHIND THE PRINTED TEXTS (*cont.*)

ways and means: memorial reconstruction, including quotation from a number of different plays; access to one or more individual actors' parts or to a theatrical 'plat' (recording the overall structure of the play and actors' entrances); note-taking or stenography during a performance. Whatever method or methods used, there will inevitably be gaps and these have to be filled in with new writing. Most critics agree that the 1603 Quarto of *Hamlet,* and the Quarto versions of *2* and *3 Henry VI* (published as *The First Part of the Contention* and *Richard Duke of York*) are the result of some such process. Other examples might, more contentiously, include the Quartos of *The Taming of A Shrew* (1594) and *The Troublesome Reign of King John* (1591).

Case study: the three early texts of *Hamlet*

There are three early texts of Shakespeare's *Hamlet*: the First Quarto (Q1), published in 1603; the Second Quarto (Q2), published in 1604; and the Folio (F), published in 1623. But the order in which these different versions were printed does not necessarily reflect the order in which the manuscripts behind them were written.

Both Q2 and F are recognisably by Shakespeare, but they each contain differences of many kinds. Some of these (in both texts) look like copying errors made by the printer. Some, particularly in the Folio, seem to be deliberate small refinements. Other larger differences in F introduce topical reference, or, as we shall see, reflect a change in approach to the writing of tragedy. For these reasons, I contend that Q2 represents Shakespeare's draft of the play, and F, a version that contains revisions by Shakespeare for performance.

The title page of the 1603 First Quarto (Q1), however, announces that the play had been acted by the King's Men in London, and in the universities of Oxford and Cambridge. This text is very much shorter than the other two versions of the play, and also reorders some of the scenes, notably bringing forward the so-called nunnery scene between Hamlet and Ophelia at 3.1 so that it precedes Hamlet's conversation with Polonius in 2.2. This is a switch that is also sometimes made in modern productions, including Peter Brook's in 2001.

In general, Q1 presents a fast-moving revenge tragedy with little of the reflection that we normally associate with Hamlet's character from our familiarity with modern editions of the play. It has had some very successful productions (notably by the Orange Tree Theatre in Richmond in 1985). But its verse is clunky and unrhythmic: 'To be, or not to be, ay there's the point, / To die, to sleep, is that all? Ay all'. It has been suggested that this version of the play was put together by two jobbing actors, not sharers in the company, who had taken the minor roles Bernardo and Marcellus while the company was on tour; it does not report the passages that only occur in the Second Quarto, while the scenes in which those characters feature are the closest to their counterparts in other versions of the play. In other words, they remembered what they could of the version they had acted, and cobbled together the bits in between. This version of the play is interesting for us, however, because of the glimpses it gives of early staging: in her mad scene, Ophelia enters '*playing on a lute, with her hair down, singing*' – any of which behaviours in public might indicate a loss of propriety in a noblewoman – while the ghost visits Gertrude's closet dressed '*in his nightgown*', perhaps in reality his shroud.

But it would not be surprising if Shakespeare had been annoyed or distressed by the circulation of this version of the play under his name, hence the publication the following year of the Second Quarto (Q2). The Q2 title page states that it is

'Newly imprinted and enlarged to almost as much again as it was, according to the true and perfect copy'. In other words, Q1 represents a corrupted, later version of the play. There is general agreement amongst scholars that *Hamlet* Q2 derives from an authorial draft of the play. Whether or not he had sold the final version to the company (see p. 56), any earlier drafts of the play might still be his to dispose of, and in any case, the company might well agree that the play's continuing life in performance would benefit from a more accurate version being available in print.

Traditionally, the Folio (F) text was dismissed as a version that had been contaminated by theatre practice and most twentieth-century editions were based on Q2, amended with F readings where these were felt to be preferable, and conflated with the passages which occur only in F. More recently, editors have been divided as to which text (Q2 or F) to use as the basis for their editions.

Structures of tragedy in the texts of *Hamlet*

There are two speeches that occur in the Q2 text of *Hamlet* separated by about twenty minutes of playing time, which share some interesting characteristics. They are both absent from the Folio text of the play and there is also no vestige of them in Q1, which suggests that they did not form part of the play in performance. They both occur immediately before entrances by the Ghost (at 1.1.125, and 1.4.38) and both end in somewhat garbled form; they do not make complete sense and, whenever they are included in modern editions, editors need to make emendations. The first speech is spoken by Hamlet's friend Horatio, and likens the presence of the Ghost who is stalking the battlements at Elsinore to the 'sheeted dead' seen in the streets of Rome before the assassination of Julius Caesar. In other words, ghosts are portents of evil deeds to come, and this speech is about the influence of the supernatural in men's lives. The second speech is Hamlet's in which he reflects on the excessive drinking habits of the Danes as a moral fault that detracts from their other good attributes. This is a speech about tragic flaw, the single fault in a person's character that causes his or her downfall.

Taken together, the absence of these two speeches from the Folio indicates that someone, presumably Shakespeare, has been rethinking the way to write tragedy. Perhaps the reason why neither speech makes syntactical sense, and why both are cut from F, is that he was encountering logical problems in trying to combine a realistic psychological approach to Hamlet's story with the traditional recipe for tragedy writing, with its supernatural influences and flawed hero.

In neither version does the Ghost tell Hamlet more than he already suspects – that his uncle murdered his father. Being a properly educated student, and a thoughtful human being, Hamlet is not, in any case, going to take such telling as proof. Being Shakespeare's creation, he puts on a play. This play, *The Murder of Gonzago*, is meant to be old-fashioned in poetic expression, acting, dramatic structure, and in its psychology, and is preceded by a dumbshow. Unlike the dumbshows of other Elizabethan plays, however, this one appears to duplicate the play that follows. Normally, a dumbshow would either present a simple emblematic image, or convey a melodramatic plot detail such as a murder, which would not then be repeated in dialogue form. But between dumbshow and play, Hamlet inserts his own threat. He announces to the king his uncle that the murderer in the play before them is 'nephew to the king' (3.2.238). Dumbshow and play are no longer identical; one has shown the past, the other is the future.

As so often, Shakespeare the playwright gives us more than one reason for events. Although Hamlet has 'heard' that 'guilty creatures, sitting at a play' can see their own story depicted and give themselves away (2.2.585), only a very inept and foolish creature would see the commonplaces of murder and adultery in a palpable work of fiction and confess his or her crimes. Claudius is neither inept nor foolish, but Hamlet's identification of the murderer as 'nephew' has told him that Hamlet intends to kill him. Hamlet exultingly takes Claudius's call for lights, and his abrupt exit, as the proof of guilt. It may be no such thing. An actor playing the part of Claudius might prefer to think of it simply as an outburst of rage at Hamlet's threat and insubordination. The next time we see Claudius, he is organising Hamlet's departure for England, where he intends him to be executed.

After the play, Hamlet comes across Claudius praying. He thinks about murdering him there and then but decides against it; he says he does not want to kill him when there is a risk of his soul going to heaven. But later, in his mother's closet, a private room for study and reflection – not, as in so many productions, a bedchamber – he hears the noise of someone behind the arras, or tapestry wall hanging. Assuming it to be Claudius, he stabs and kills this person, who turns out to be Polonius, father of the woman he loves. Before hauling the dead body away, Hamlet reminds his mother that he is being sent to England. It is only in the Q2 text that he tells her and us that he is to be accompanied by his erstwhile friends, Rosencrantz and Guildenstern, whom he intends, somehow, to have killed:

> There's letters sealed; and my two schoolfellows,
> Whom I will trust as I will adders fanged,
> They bear the mandate; they must sweep my way
> And marshal me to knavery. Let it work,
> For 'tis the sport to have the enginer
> Hoist with his own petard ...
>
> (3.4.202–7)

Shortly afterwards, on his way to take ship, and again only in the Q2 text, he encounters the army of young Fortinbras. This young man has given up his attempt to recapture lands, lost by his father the King of Norway during single combat with Hamlet's father, and is now off to conquer part of Poland instead. Fortinbras's captain tells Hamlet that the land itself is not worth a straw, let alone the deaths of 20,000 people, but this nevertheless prompts Hamlet's seventh soliloquy, 'How all occasions do inform against me', in which he compares himself unfavourably with Fortinbras and berates himself for not taking his revenge against Claudius.

The problem of course, in terms of play construction, is that the last few scenes have been full of action. Hamlet has threatened Claudius, decided on his guilt, and killed someone that in the heat of the moment he believed to be him. Since that disastrous mistake there has been no time for a more considered revenge. So there are logical difficulties in the plot and the writing of the Q2 text. These are mostly removed in the F text. In that version, Hamlet cheerfully takes his leave of his mother, having killed the meddling minister, but without planning to murder anyone else. Once he has been dispatched for England we do not see him again until his return. We briefly see Fortinbras's army trudge across the stage, but Hamlet's dialogue with the captain and his seventh soliloquy are both cut. And with them go all the evidence that critics commonly adduce as proof of Hamlet's tragic flaw of delay.

Now, we no longer have to tell ourselves that of course the Elizabethans believed in revenge (which, of course, they did not, since it is a recipe for civil disorder and therefore dangerous to the state). Hamlet himself is no more unhinged or illogical than any of us might be if we were living under the same roof as an uncle who had married our mother and whom we suspected had murdered our father. And he is no more paralysed into inaction than any of us would be were we living in a state where friends are employed to spy on us, and where the only arbiter of justice is also the criminal we would wish to see indicted. And yet, he has rejected his lover and murdered her father, and later, before he has time to think, he will be responsible for sending Rosencrantz and Guildenstern to their deaths. His life is a mess. This is the real tragedy of *Hamlet*, and one that comes over much more clearly in the Folio text once the literary convention of tragic flaw is removed: that under corrupt governments, terrible things happen to decent people, and they in turn can sometimes do terrible things to others.

The texts of Shakespeare's plays are thus not as fixed as they appear to be, and the different versions offer very different possibilities for meaning and interpretation. This is not a case of all interpretations being equally valid. Rather it is a case of someone, presumably in this particular case Shakespeare, reshaping the text to create a different set of causes and effects. There is a real, politically important tragedy in the Folio version of *Hamlet*, which is present but unhelpfully obscured in Q2 by the concepts and structural elements of traditional tragic form. The two texts of Shakespeare's *Hamlet* thus show us a mind at work on a set of artistic problems not only connected with the writing of tragedy, but with the expression of perennially important ethical problems.

PRINTING DATES FOR SHAKESPEAREAN QUARTOS AND OCTAVOS PRIOR TO THE PUBLICATION OF THE 1623 FOLIO, WITH THEIR TITLE PAGE ATTRIBUTIONS TO ACTING COMPANIES

1591 *The Troublesome Reign of King John* (i.e. a play similar in structure to *King John*); Queen's

1594 *The First Part of the Contention betwixt the Two Famous Houses of York and Lancaster* (i.e. a shortened version of 2 *Henry VI*, reprinted 1600, 1619)

PRINTING DATES FOR SHAKESPEAREAN QUARTOS AND OCTAVOS PRIOR TO THE PUBLICATION OF THE 1623 FOLIO, WITH THEIR TITLE PAGE ATTRIBUTIONS TO ACTING COMPANIES (*cont.*)

The Taming of a Shrew (i.e. a play with some resemblance to *The Taming of The Shrew*, reprinted 1596, 1607); Pembroke's

Titus Andronicus (reprinted 1600, 1611); Derby's, Pembroke's, and Sussex's; the 1600 edition adds Chamberlain's

The True Tragedy of Richard III (a play about Richard III, but not similar to Shakespeare's); Queen's

1595 *The True Tragedy of Richard Duke of York* (a version of 3 *Henry VI*, reprinted 1600, 1619); Pembroke's

1597 *Richard II* (reprinted 1598, twice; 1608, 1615); Chamberlain's

1598 *Richard III* (reprinted 1602, 1605, 1609, 1612, 1622); Chamberlain's

Romeo and Juliet (reprinted 1599, 1609, 1622); Chamberlain's

1 *Henry IV* (reprinted 1599, 1604, 1608, 1613, 1622)

Loves Labours Lost

1600 2 *Henry IV;* Chamberlain's

Henry V (reprinted 1602, 1619); Chamberlain's

The Merchant of Venice (reprinted 1619, but falsely dated 1600); Chamberlain's

A Midsummer Night's Dream (reprinted 1619, falsely dated 1600); Chamberlain's

Much Ado About Nothing; Chamberlain's

1602 *Merry Wives of Windsor* (reprinted 1619); Chamberlain's

1603 *Hamlet* (Q1); King's

1604 *Hamlet* (Q2, reprinted 1611, and subsequently with no date)

1608 *King Lear* (reprinted 1619, but falsely dated 1608); King's

1609 *Pericles* (twice; reprinted 1611, 1619); King's

Troilus and Cressida

1622 *Othello;* King's

2

Shakespeare and the theatre business

If the tag-rag people did not clap him and hiss him, according as he pleased and displeased them, as they use to do the players in the theatre, I am no true man.

(*Julius Caesar*, 1.2.257–60)

The previous chapter outlined the main trajectory of Shakespeare's life and career, and considered Shakespeare in print. It did not, though, speculate as to how Shakespeare could have achieved the status of sharer in the main playing company of his day by the time he was thirty, nor how, at the age of thirty-three, he had become sufficiently wealthy to have bought a large and comfortable house in his home town. This early part of Shakespeare's career is highly contentious, but it is important to our understanding of his development as a dramatist that we try to untangle it. In order to tell some kind of rational story, we need to look at the context in which he was working as an actor and dramatist, and therefore the ways in which the theatre of his time operated and was financed. There were no 'rules' governing this, and historians have often made the mistake of discussing theatre practices as if there were. This was a commercial enterprise, and actors, writers, and theatre owners alike were all entrepreneurs. Inevitably, some were more successful than others, but all would have seized the opportunity to make money where and when they could.

The records of expenditure on play production at court for this period are scattered through the financial accounts of the various offices of the royal households. From the Chamber accounts, we learn that a single performance at court at the end of the sixteenth century would earn a company of actors £10. The works accounts record the costs of transforming the great halls of the various royal palaces into temporary theatres; and the accounts of the Revels Office which was responsible for props and costumes for court masques and other shows, and for vetting and censoring stage plays, show the costs involved in making, storing, and repairing the props and costumes they owned. These records are all incomplete. Different individuals had different accounting practices, and often only end of year summaries survive. Thomas Cawarden, Master of the Revels in the early years of Elizabeth's reign, however, personally preserved endless bills and debentures, sometimes no more than tiny scraps of paper recording the purchase of bolts of cloth, and accessories such as feathers and wigs. These were kept by his descendants at the family home, Loseley House in Surrey, for three hundred years before being (mostly) sold to the Folger Shakespeare Library in Washington. They give us a wonderfully detailed feel for the workings of the Revels Office at that period, although they usually reveal little about particular plays or entertainments.

Glimpses of companies of actors on tour in the provinces can be found in the financial accounts of local civic authorities, and in surviving household account books. These usually do not name the play. Like the court records, the function of these documents is to track expenditure rather than to record the plays or the practice of playing in itself. Such records need interpretation. Sometimes, the payment is to the company to get them to go away and not to perform. This has often been interpreted as evidence of anti-theatricality in the countryside, although it might suggest the opposite – that the company would normally have expected to play a particular town and was being compensated for loss of income because of the unforeseen prohibition. Income direct from sales would not go through the local authority's books, which would only record special performances paid for by the town council. Much of the normal practice of public playing may therefore be invisible to us now.

Most of what we know about the economics and practicalities of early modern play production in London's public theatres is gleaned from the 'diary', or rather account books and other papers, of Philip Henslowe. In addition to his three theatres – the Rose, the Fortune, and a theatre to the south of London at Newington Butts – he was part-owner with his son-in-law, the actor Edward Alleyn, of the bear-baiting ring on Bankside. Henslowe's financial records of course only give us a partial picture – the theatre owner's view – and they do not record the same types of item consistently over time. Nevertheless, they afford some fascinating glimpses of his theatrical, money-lending, and other businesses, while his daily itemised receipts in the early 1590s listing every play performed by title reveal the repertoires of several theatre companies who played in his theatre, including the companies with which Shakespeare was probably involved.

From October 1597, Henslowe also seems to have acted as a kind of banker to the company in residence in his theatre, the Admiral's Men, regularly lending them money to buy costumes or to pay writers for plays. Later, when the Admiral's Men moved to the Fortune, the Rose was occupied by Worcester's Men, and Henslowe continued to lend to them. Shakespeare's own money-lending activities in Stratford have prompted speculation that he may have performed a similar banking service for the Chamberlain's Men, although there is no positive evidence for this.

In fact there is no record at all of day-to-day income and expenditure for the companies to which Shakespeare is known to have belonged at the Theatre or the Globe. While it is useful to look at the theatre practices represented by Henslowe's financial records, we must bear in mind that not all theatre companies were owned or operated in the same way. The Chamberlain's Men was a joint stock company with a number of sharers, while Shakespeare himself, from 1594 onwards, is unique in being an actor, writer, and part-owner of the company (and later the theatre) in which he worked.

MONEY AND COSTS

£1 = 20s (shillings) = 240d (pennies)
1s = 12d
1d = 2 halfpennies or ha'pennies
groat = small silver coin of variable weight and value, but later equivalent to 4d.

In *1 Henry IV*, Falstaff has consumed a loaf of bread costing 1/2d, a capon at 2s 2d, and two gallons of sack or sherry, 5s 8d.

A skilled artisan might earn 12d per day, or 6s for a six-day week.

A Swiss visitor to London, Thomas Platter, tells us that the cost of a standing place in the yard at one of the London public playhouses in 1599 was one penny (1d). Patrons who desired the shelter of the galleries, where they might also sit, would pay a further 1d to the door keeper, while access to the gentlemen's rooms or boxes either side of the stage at first floor level, and the lords' room in the tiring house over the stage at the back, offered more comfort and exclusivity for corresponding fees. Excavations at the Rose Theatre uncovered shards of pottery money-jars used by such door keepers.

Theatre companies, plays, and playwrights

In 1591 Henslowe records regular weekly payments to 'Mr Tyllnes man'. Edward Tilney was Master of the Revels at court, and also responsible for licensing the public theatres. Later these payments become fortnightly, and then monthly, and appear to be payments for a license for the theatre, although other payments to Tilney in the accounts are for individual play licenses. In 1597, Henslowe made a loan of seven shillings to one of the actors to cover the cost of a play licence. A new play, and any play that had been revised with new material, needed its own individual licence. This would be written on the manuscript itself, and could be shown to civic authorities in the country when the company was on tour, proving that the play was approved and allowed for public performance. This is probably the reason why selected performances in Henslowe's records are marked by him as 'ne'. This cannot mean simply 'new' as is sometimes suggested, since the anonymous play *Alexander and Lodowick* is designated thus on two separate occasions. It probably means newly licensed (or relicensed), or rather perhaps 'newly entered' in the Revels Office register of allowed plays, for there must have been some such official record kept in the Revels Office itself which has not survived. The fact of 'newness' or of being newly revised and improved was, of course, also a marketing tool, and Henslowe's takings are usually significantly higher for these performances.

From Henslowe's papers, we learn that a company might own the play books in its repertoire corporately, and deduce that both Henslowe and Alleyn bought plays as individuals. Play titles are seen to recur in the repertoires of different companies playing in Henslowe's theatres, and once or twice Alleyn sells on a play, personally recouping £2.

Among his lists of performances, many of which recall plays that are now lost, Henslowe's book includes his receipts for performances of plays which we know to have been by Marlowe – *Doctor Faustus, The Jew of Malta,* and *Tamburlaine,* for instance – and also for Thomas Kyd's popular revenge play *The Spanish Tragedy.* Later, in his 'banker' phase, there are payments and advances to a number of different authors for additions to old plays such as those in order to keep them current, as well as for new work. Some of the more lurid titles include *The Blind Eats Many a Fly* by Thomas Heywood, and *The Black Dog of Newgate* (both for Worcester's Men). The latter necessitated the purchase of lambskins and a suit of canvas, presumably to make the dog costume. Actors would be expected to supply their own playing clothes for most purposes, and only costumes for special effects would be provided by the company.

This play was popular enough for its team of four writers to be paid £7 for an immediate sequel; the usual price varied between £6 and £8. This would not have gone very far when shared between two or more co-authors, which the accounts show was common. Even working alone, a writer would need to be producing at least two plays a year to earn the equivalent of a skilled artisan's wages.

COSTUMES

Costume designer and historian Jenny Tiramani stresses that Elizabethan players wore real clothes, not mocked-up costumes, and followed this principle in her designs for the Shakespeare's Globe Theatre productions in its initial seasons. One outfit might consist of more than twenty separate items, including shift; bodice; separate sleeves; separate cuffs; ruff or collar; underskirts; overskirt etc., all held together with ties and pins. Cloth was a valuable commodity and there was a thriving market in second-hand clothes, as can be seen from the pages of Henslowe's account book. Tourist Thomas Platter writes:

> The comedians are most expensively and elegantly apparelled since it is customary in England, when distinguished gentlemen or knights die, for nearly the finest of their clothes to be made over and given to their servants, and as it is not proper for them to wear such clothes but only to imitate them, they give them to the comedians to purchase for a small sum.

COSTUMES (*cont.*)

The only contemporary picture showing Elizabethan actors dressed for a performance of a Shakespeare play relates to *Titus Andronicus*, although it does not correspond precisely to any one scene. This drawing, by Henry Peacham, is in the library of the Marquis of Bath at Longleat. Like the picture of the Swan, it is probably a composite of different points in time, since the character on the right of the picture, Aaron the Moor, is slightly out of the plane, and is pointing out the others. The scene shows Titus in a Roman toga, a couple of soldiers dressed as Elizabethan guards, and Tamora in a gown that is neither classical nor Elizabethan, but suggests her status as queen and exotic foreigner. Similar mixtures of costumes from different periods have been used to great effect in many modern productions of Shakespeare.

Companies resident in a theatre needed a constant supply of new plays in order to keep their local audiences entertained. There were usually six performances each week, and a different play every day. The playwrights regularly hired at the Rose were churning them out – an industrial production of scripts not unlike what we find in the film and TV industries today. Henslowe often paid (and the playwrights might deliver) in instalments, beginning with a 'plot', outlining the arrangement of the scenes, their principal characters, and any major effects. In cases of multiple authorship, the plot might also serve as a plan for dividing up the writing. Henslowe's account books show us that it was a common practice at this time for one person to be responsible for setting out the plot of a play so that it could be farmed out to others for the actual writing. Indeed, this is still a common practice where teams of writers are involved in producing drama series or films. From Henslowe's lists of play titles we can see that the repertoire at the Rose also consisted of the same mix of romance, horror, and historical drama, including the occasional bible story, and the same desire to capitalise on a money-spinning formula that we now associate with Hollywood.

The completed script would be read to the assembled company, and then there might be a three-week gap for learning the play before the first performance. First, the play would have to be copied. The company would not afford the time or the paper to be able to do this in its entirety for each actor. Instead, for each character he was playing, an actor would be given a part, a scroll or roll of paper – hence the term 'role' – on which was written all the speeches for the character, with each speech preceded by up to three words of cue. The process of role and roll distribution and rehearsal is demonstrated comically in *A Midsummer Night's Dream*, where the inexperienced Flute the bellows mender speaks all his part 'at once, cues and all' (3.1.90). Alleyn's part for Orlando in Robert Greene's *Orlando Furioso* survives among the Henslowe papers. The practice was usual throughout Europe from the medieval period until at least the end of the eighteenth century.

It might be thought that if the actor can only read his own part he will find the play more difficult to understand. But it does force him to listen acutely while waiting for his cue, and thus contributes to good ensemble playing. Perhaps it is also easier for him to keep track of what his character knows at any given point in the play if he is not confused by reading what the other characters know. Overall, this may make the business of performing that character rather easier.

1592: Strange's Men and *1 Henry VI*

If Shakespeare were a member of Strange's company in the late 1580s or early 1590s, his real value to them would have been as a writer rather than an actor. The company had previously performed only sporadically at court, being paid mostly for feats of juggling and tumbling. Suddenly, however, they start appearing there regularly, and are being paid not for acrobatics but for plays: two in the winter of 1590–1 and six in 1591–2. Part of this success is undoubtedly because star actor Edward Alleyn had joined them, even though he retained his identity as servant to Lord Howard, the Lord Admiral. But actors need words. Could he have been attracted to them because they had acquired the services of a very different, rising young dramatist?

The two companies, Strange's and Admiral's, are found playing together in provincial tours all over the country for the next two years. Between March and June (and again in December 1592), they were at the Rose Theatre on Bankside. Henslowe records approximately twenty-five plays in their repertoire; the precise figure is difficult to determine because of his tendency to refer to the same play by different names. Nine plays are given only once. Some of the plays would have been in the repertoire for some time, but whether learning new or reviving old, the feat of memory is considerable, and the time available for rehearsal extremely limited.

There are, however, an unprecedented sixteen or again, since Henslowe is not precise as to titles, perhaps even seventeen performances of a play he calls *Harey the VI*. It outperforms every other play in the repertoire except perhaps Thomas Kyd's *The Spanish Tragedy* (again, depending on one's interpretation of the various titles that Henslowe uses for what might be one or at most two plays, *The Spanish Tragedy* itself, and its prequel, *The First Part of Hieronimo*). Henslowe's receipts usually amounted to slightly over £1 and sometimes more than £3, although they could be as little as three shillings on a particularly bad afternoon. The seventeen performances of *Harey the VI* net him just under £35 – considerably more than his average takings for that number of performances. It is probable that this play is what we now know as Shakespeare's *Henry VI* part one, because in a satire entitled *Pierce Penniless his Supplication to the Devil* (published in 1592 and entered in the Stationers' Register on 8 August that year), Thomas Nash describes the recent outstanding success of 'famous Ned Alleyn' as Talbot, the lead character in Shakespeare's play.

The first part of *Henry VI* may well be a prequel written after the success of the plays we now know as parts two and three. Recent productions of all three plays directed by Michael Boyd for the Royal Shakespeare Company demonstrated how thrilling they can still be in performance. The ebb and flow of the fortunes of the opposed York and Lancaster factions in England's first civil war, the Wars of the Roses, is hugely exciting when performed energetically.

But these are not just 'history plays' about quarrelling noblemen and the loss of sovereignty over France. They would have had particular political significance to Elizabethans, who were divided along religious lines, and under threat from foreign invasion. Jack Cade's grass roots rebellion is the central event in part two, while in part three, the grim, pointless reality of civil war is summed up in the terrible symmetry of a single stage direction: 'Enter a son that hath killed his father at one door, and a father that hath killed his son at another door' (2.5.54-124). King Henry looks on as each man in turn discovers what he has done and, grieving, anticipates the endless grief of mother and wife.

The sense that these are plays about England and that England is the sum of its people is particularly strong in part one, and especially in the character of Talbot. Noted as a great military hero, with an old-fashioned sense of chivalric honour, he was, in life, both violent and quarrelsome. As a character in this play, however, he represents the best of England, betrayed by the squabbles and rivalries of the country's leaders, and is humanised as a man with a son whom he loves deeply, and whom he tries to save from the consequences of inevitable defeat. In the event, father and son die, movingly, in each other's arms.

The spectacular use of the whole theatre building required by *1 Henry VI* must have wowed its first audiences and might in itself account for the enormous success of *Harey the VI*. All the levels of the stage and tiering house structure are used. Just before her capture, Joan is attended by a set of melancholy devils who would have appeared from a trapdoor in the stage floor. The balcony over the stage and the stage entrance doors below become the lookouts and gates of a succession of fortresses and walled towns. At one point Joan enters a town secretly in disguise as a peasant going to market. She exits the stage through the stage doors, representing the gates of the town, but she then reappears '*thrusting out a torch burning*' to give the signal for the French to attack '*on the top*' (3.3.6) – presumably the place in the turret high above the stage, where a trumpeter would normally announce to the surrounding streets the imminent start of a play. Burning torches are always exciting (and dangerous) props in performance. In another scene, Salisbury and Talbot are found talking '*on the turrets*' where they can 'overpeer the city' of Orleans, while the French master gunner's boy crosses the stage below '*with a linstock*' to fire the cannon that then blows away the side of Salisbury's head (1.4). English soldiers storm the walls with '*scaling ladders, their drums beating a dead march*' after which the French, surprised in their sleep, '*leap o'er the walls in their shirts*', their leaders rendered ridiculous by being '*half ready and half unready*' (2.1.8–48).

Even apart from the cannon fire, it is a very noisy play. Joan is several times accompanied by thunder and lightning; the English shout their battle cry 'A Talbot! A Talbot!'; groups meet skirmishing with a clash of steel. Opposing forces in succession march across the stage with trumpet flourishes, drums, and colours; they are beaten back with alarums, excursions, and retreats, before flourishes announce the other side's victory. Many in the audience would know these drum and trumpet signals from recent first hand experience of battlefields in France or the Netherlands, or from military exercises and musters on the exercise grounds of Finsbury Fields or Mile End. And there are two very feisty, arresting, and witty female characters: Joan herself, and Margaret, daughter of King Reignier, who will marry Henry VI. Whether in staging, the range of language spoken, the mixture of emotion, suspense, humour, excitement, and pathos, or the novel approach to women, there had been nothing else quite like it in the history of English drama.

The panache of this structure probably confirms that it was conceived and plotted by Shakespeare – justifying its inclusion by his friends Hemmings and Condell in the collected edition of his works. But the play may not have been entirely *written* by him. Recent statistical linguistic analysis by Hugh Craig and Arthur Kinney exploring the frequency of certain word usage in different sections of the play may indicate that the Joan of Arc scenes were written by Christopher Marlowe, and the first act of the play by Thomas Nash. According to their analysis, however, Shakespeare wrote 'almost all of the action involving Lord Talbot' (Craig and Kinney 2009, p. 51).

This division of the writing, and also Shakespeare's possible role as conceiver, manager, and owner of the entire project, might understandably have led to some professional rivalry felt by university-educated Nash for the actor Shakespeare. This might explain why Nash's eulogy on Ned Alleyn's performance conveys some rather snide comments on the structure and reception of the Talbot scenes of the play, and of playacting in general:

> How would it have joyed brave Talbot (the terror of the French) to think that after he had lain two hundred years in his tomb he should triumph again on the stage, and have his bones new embalmed with the tears of ten thousand spectators at least (at several times) who in the tragedian that represents his person, imagine they behold him fresh bleeding? ... there is no immortality can be given to man on earth like unto plays.
>
> (Pierce Penniless)

Nash is always slippery. The apparently ringing endorsement of the modern fashion for history plays which, he says, are drawn from 'our English Chronicles' and therefore moral, educative, and patriotic, is not unqualified. Talbot had in fact been killed at the battle of Castillon in 1453, one hundred and thirty-nine years previously, not two hundred. Is Nash knowingly alluding to the ahistoricism of a play that shows Talbot dead at the feet of Joan of Arc who had been burnt at the stake in 1431? This and the bracketed 'at several times' alert the reader to the hyperbolic tendentiousness, even impossibility, of the claim 'no immortality can be given to man on earth like unto plays'. A few lines later these sly doubts have materialised into a very backhanded defence of the value of theatre: if war plays are popular, it must be because most of the audience is made up of idle soldiery and other layabouts.

> For whereas the after-noon being the idlest time of the day; wherein men that are their own masters (as gentlemen of the court, the Inns of the Court, and the number of captains and soldiers about London) do wholly bestow themselves upon pleasure, and that pleasure they divide (how virtuously it skills not) either into gaming, following of harlots, drinking, or seeing a play, is it not then better (since of four extremes all the world cannot keep them but they will choose one) that they should betake them to the least, which is plays?

1592: the 'upstart crow'

Nash and Marlowe, along with the dramatist George Peele, are all addressed together in a letter appended to a more overt and much more famous attack on Shakespeare, a pamphlet entitled *Greene's Groatsworth of Wit*, which refers to one 'Shake-scene' as an 'upstart crow', and theatre's 'Jack of all trades'. This book was entered in the Stationers' Register in September 1592, just one month after *Pierce Penniless*, and published that same year. It is the earliest and also most controversial reference to Shakespeare as both actor and playwright.

The full title of this book is *Greene's Groatsworth of Wit, bought with a million of repentance. Describing the folly of youth, the falsehood of makeshift flatterers, the misery of the negligent, and mischiefs of deceiving courtesans. Written before his death, and published at his dying request.* Some four years older than Shakespeare, Robert Greene had died in penury in August that year, apparently of a surfeit of herrings and Rhenish wine, shortly before publication of the book. He had had particular success with romantic comedies, and plays that mixed romance and history, although the bulk of his output as a writer consisted of satirical pamphlets and 'prose romances' – effectively early novels. His popular romantic comedy *Friar Bacon and Friar Bungay* was also in Strange's repertoire alongside *Harey the VI* during that Rose season, as was his *Looking-glass for London and England*, which he had written in collaboration with Thomas Lodge, and a single performance of his *Orlando Furioso*. He had been trying to secure the patronage of Lord Strange, so perhaps there were a number of reasons for him to be jealous of the younger man's success.

Whether Greene was in fact the author, however, is uncertain; it is possible that the *Groatsworth* was actually written by Henry Chettle or perhaps, again, Thomas Nash, since it contains some echoes of other works by Nash. Chettle was soon in print denying that he and Nash had had any involvement with it, while Nash too publicly disavowed it. I shall use the name 'Greene' for convenience.

'Greene's' objective in this work is to warn his friends. All of them, he says, will suffer, through their acquaintance with unkind, untrustworthy actors:

> Base minded men all three of you, if by my misery you be not
> warned, for unto none of you (like me) sought those burrs to
> cleave – those puppets (I mean) that spake from our mouths,
> those antics garnished in our colours. Is it not strange, that I, to
> whom they all have been beholding: is it not like that you, to
> whom they all have been beholding, shall (were ye in that case
> as I am now) be both at once of them forsaken? Yes trust them
> not; for there is an upstart crow, beautified with our feathers,
> that with his *Tigers heart wrapped in a player's hide*, supposes he is
> as well able to bombast out a blank verse as the best of you, and
> being an absolute *Johannes factotum*, is in his own conceit the
> only Shake-scene in a country. O that I might entreat your rare
> wits to be employed in more profitable courses, & let those apes
> imitate your past excellence, and never more acquaint them
> with your admired inventions … yet whilst you may, seek you
> better masters; for it is pity men of such rare wits, should be
> subject to the pleasure of such rude grooms.

Both the identification of this 'Shake-scene' with Shakespeare,
and the prior existence of the third part of the *Henry VI* plays are
confirmed by the *Groatsworth*'s parody of the line 'a tiger's heart
wrapped in a woman's hide', spoken by the rebel Duke of York
to Queen Margaret (*3 Henry VI*, 1.4.137). She has captured him
and has waved in his face a handkerchief which she says is
drenched in the blood of his youngest son, a mere child, whom
we have previously seen with his tutor moments before his
death. The atrocities committed by both sides in this civil war
have been equal and opposite, but the murder of a child and the
desecration of a body by a woman is still more shocking to most
people than the equivalent acts committed by a man. 'Greene'
uses York's disgust to attack Shake-scene.

Greene never lost an opportunity to designate himself as
Master of Arts, and his tract is usually interpreted as simple
resentment of the fact that Shakespeare the actor has taken up

writing. Recently, however, critics have tended to revert to the older interpretation that 'Greene' is accusing Shakespeare of plagiarism or 'patching up' the work of other writers. Most accounts concentrate their attention on the line 'upstart crow beautified with our feathers'. Few examine the language of the passage as a whole or its classical literary allusions. Even fewer place this outburst within the wider context of the book, and none notices that that context (as indeed indicated in the second word of the title) is not so much about art and authorship as about money and class: proper writers, 'Greene' believes, have had a university education; they are therefore, by definition, gentlemen, but they are also, invariably, poor.

The book contains a number of references to writers being ripped off by actors – 'puppets' who make comfortable livings through speaking their words. An actor would be paid every time he set foot on a stage. A playwright would normally get nothing beyond his initial fee for a script, no matter how success-ful his play. There were no performing rights, and no copyright or royalties on the sale of printed books; in Britain, performing rights for dramatists date only from the Dramatic Literary Property Act of 1833. In 1619, the poet and playwright Ben Jonson told his friend William Drummond of Hawthornden that he had earned less than £200 in twenty years of the work. Once Jonson or Greene, or any of their fellows, sold a play to an individual actor like Alleyn, or to an acting company, it became the exclusive property of that actor or company, and the writer could expect no further income from it.

'Greene' describes a dying usurer who leaves all his wealth to his younger son, giving just a groat to his university-educated older son, perhaps not accidentally called Roberto, to buy a 'groatsworth of wit'. The book tells how Roberto ruins his brother and is then approached by an extremely well-dressed person who tells him 'men of my profession get by scholars their whole living'. Roberto asks what profession that might be and is surprised to learn he is a player, thinking from his appearance he was 'a Gentleman of great living':

> 'So am I where I dwell', quoth the player, 'reputed able at my proper cost to build a windmill. What though the world once went hard with me, when I was fain to carry my playing fardle a footback, *tempora mutantur*, I know you know the meaning of it better than I, but I thus conster it, it's otherwise now, for my very share in playing apparel will not be sold for two hundred pounds.'

> 'Truly', said *Roberto*, ''tis strange, that you should so prosper in that vain practice, for that it seems to me your voice is nothing gracious.'

The satire flies around; two hundred pounds is an outrageously large sum for an actor's stock of play clothes. Theatres, as we have seen, were located in the suburbs, country regions where windmills were found, as shown on an early printed panorama of London known as the Agas map (*c.* 1562). These were places close enough to the city for their clientele to access them, but outside the jurisdiction of the city's Lord Mayor and aldermen. 'Greene's' actor is a country bumpkin, a miller (a proverbially dishonest profession), relatively ignorant of Latin and certainly less well educated than Roberto. Like Roberto's father the usurer, he started out with nothing and has made a fortune – with the implication that he has done that, as usurers do, by exploiting other people. He has a bad voice to boot. The player has formerly written plays himself, but his moral style is out of date, and so he offers to employ Roberto as a playwright, 'for which you shall be well paid, if you will take the pains'. Tarlton – lead actor of the Queen's Men – cultivated a stage persona as a country rustic, and had written a play called *The Seven Deadly Sins*. In attacking a Tarlton-like figure, 'Greene' is attacking the archetypal actor.

The image of the crow in the direct attack on Shakespeare, however, is perhaps a combination of two of Aesop's fables, known in England at the time through their use in satires and odes by the Roman poet Horace. In one, a jackdaw (a species of crow) steals the dropped feathers of a number of other birds to make himself a new plumage. Jove is impressed by his spectacular appearance and makes him king of birds, whereupon the other birds turn on him, pecking out both the feathers he has stolen and his own. The moral seems to be 'don't pretend to be what you're not'. Horace uses this story in Epistle 1.3 as an injunction not to borrow the writings of others. The other is the fable about the fox and the crow. This begins with the observation that anyone who listens to flatterers is a fool and will end his days in repentance – as the persona 'Greene' is 'repenting' in the title of this, his end-of-life rant. A crow sits in a tree with a tasty cheese in his beak. A fox comes by and remarks on the beauty of his feathers: if only his voice were as beautiful, there would be no bird like him. The crow, is flattered, opens his beak to sing, and lets fall the cheese, which is seized by the fox.

The word 'upstart' could have two senses: a newcomer or parvenue, or someone who engages in 'newfangledness' (a term of disapproval often used by Nash for writers who experiment with new or fashionable styles of writing). 'Greene's' fellow playwrights, like Aesop's crow, have been flattered into giving away their work to the actors, while Shake-scene, the actor-turned-writer, is taking the bread out of the mouths of proper writers, appropriating both cheese and feathers – a wily fox in crow's clothing, perhaps, with the heart of a ravening tiger. Not content to be an actor (and perhaps not a particularly good actor either) earning money every time he steps on a stage, Shake-scene is a *Johannes factotum*, Jack of all trades: actor, writer, and perhaps, given the book's insistence on money, a 'factor', or agent, for the theatre companies, a buyer and seller of other writers' work. The complaint is very similar to Nash's in *Pierce Penniless*. It too supports the idea that Shakespeare was a writer of plots that have been fleshed out, or feathered up, by other (better) writers, while the scenes he has contributed himself are extravagantly rhetorical. It is an explosion of jealousy for someone who, unlike 'Greene', seems to be finding a way of making the theatre pay.

By interpreting the comment about stealing feathers as a complaint that Shakespeare was a plagiarist, critics and biographers have used the *Groatsworth* to support the position that Shakespeare had only just begun writing in 1592, and was being employed as a 'play patcher', a reviser of other men's work – although why any company would ask an unknown, untried writer to make improvements to established works is never explained. The phrase 'to patch up' a text at this period more commonly means putting together quotations from different authors and perhaps adding a gloss of one's own; it is used by writers on both sides of the religious divide to attack each other's theology; as Thomas Harding expressed it in 1567, 'to corrupte, to patche together, to mangle, and by other waies to falsifie'. There are plenty of early modern plays that appear to have been put together in that way, but Shakespeare's are not among them. Shakespeare, it seems to me, was acting as a producer: designing and managing projects, and commissioning authors, as well as writing himself.

An early *Hamlet*

A reference to an early *Hamlet* play may also fit into this story. This play was on stage by 1589, when it was described by Thomas Nash in his preface to Robert Greene's romance *Menaphon*:

> yet English *Seneca* read by candle-light yields many good sentences, as *Blood is a beggar*, and so forth: and if you intreat him fair in a frosty morning, he will afford you whole *Hamlets*, I should say handfuls of tragical speeches. But O Grief! … what's that will last always? The sea exhaled by drops will in

> continuance be dry, and Seneca let blood line by line and page
> by page, at length must needs die to our stage; which makes his
> famished followers to imitate the kid in Aesop, who enamoured
> with the fox's new-fangles, forsook all hopes of life to leap into
> a new occupation.

Nash's preface is a wide-ranging attack on the ignorance and
conceit of actors, puffed up by performing the work of writers
who pass off imitations of Italian and classical authors as their
own invention, and chase after 'newfangledness'. It seems to
refer to the version of Aesop's tale of the wolf and the kid, also
found in the May Eclogue from Spenser's *Shepherd's Calendar*,
where a fox dressed as a peddler abducts a young kid by encouraging him to nose into his pack in search of trifles and gewgaws.
Nash is punning on the name of Thomas Kyd, author of the
bloody and popular *Spanish Tragedy*, which imitates the tragedies
of Seneca, a Roman philosopher and writer of 'sentences' or
moral sayings. He seems to be complaining that the author of
this play has not only imitated both Kyd and Seneca but is more
extreme than either.

The early *Hamlet* play is listed as performed by the
Chamberlain's Men at Newington Butts in 1594, and comes
under attack again in 1596 when Thomas Lodge, another in the
circle of university-educated writers, wrote in *Wits Misery and
the Worlds Madness: Discovering the Devils Incarnate of this Age*:

> he walks for the most part in black under colour of gravity, and
> looks as pale as the visard of the ghost which cried so miserably
> at the Theatre like an oysterwife, 'Hamlet, revenge' ...

Nash and Lodge are assuming widespread cultural understanding
of their references to this play, which suggests that it was
extremely popular. It is clearly also a play that has got under their
skin for some reason, and both seem to be annoyed about some
aspect of its interface between writing and performance. The

Theatre is where Shakespeare's company was performing at this time, and it has sometimes been suggested that he himself, even as a young actor, may have specialised in 'old man' roles, and may have taken the part of the ghost. It is generally assumed that the play in question must have been a blood and guts revenge tragedy by an anonymous writer. The current orthodoxy concerning a late start for Shakespeare's career has prevented reconsideration of the possibility that it might be an early draft of the play that we know by him. Yet the satires we have been considering by the university wits 'Greene', Nash, and Lodge all concur as attacks on plays and playwrights that court popularity through what they try to dismiss as vulgar, upstart newfangledness. There is insufficient evidence to settle this question either

REGULATING THE PRINT TRADE

In the sixteenth and seventeenth centuries, England had probably the most sophisticated system for the regulation of printing in Europe; but it was regulation originally devised by the Stationers' Company for the economic control of their own industry and the protection of their members' livelihoods – not those of authors. They were supported in this by the crown, which saw a ready-made institution for political control. Copyright, although the word did not then exist, lay with the stationer (printer and/or publisher) who had paid his sixpence to the Wardens of the Company for the licence to print a particular text. This right then formed part of his estate. He could leave it to his heirs or sell it to another stationer who would pay a corresponding fee to the Company for the transfer. Although sensitive books might be sent to representatives of the church or the Privy Council for censoring, responsibility for the content of a book lay primarily with the stationer who owned it and the Company's Wardens who licensed it, rather than with the author; and while many titles appeared anonymously, all books were supposed to carry the names of their printer and publisher.

way. But Shakespeare's acknowledged later version of *Hamlet* is above all a play about acting, in which a king admits the deceit of his 'most painted word', a company of actors are the 'chronicle' of the times, and a play is used in an attempt to establish truth. Perhaps partly as an answer to Nash and the others, that play is an enduring defence of the value of theatre.

1594: the printing of *Titus Andronicus*

Plays were (and are) ephemeral; in early-modern England, a play might not make it to a second performance, let alone into print. Although more than 800 plays were printed between 1500 and 1660, most of the dramas and entertainments of the Elizabethan period are lost. It used to be assumed that it was not in a company's interest to put a play into print, since once it was available on the bookstalls anyone could perform it. But insofar as the evidence still exists, it seems that those plays that were printed tended to appear some two or three years after the likely date of their first performance, coinciding with a revival: the play had stood the test of time; it was worth reviving; it might therefore also be worth printing. This process would be mutually beneficial for performers and printers alike, since the playbill advertising the play in performance and the presence of printed copies in the bookshops would reinforce each other commercially. This would also explain why the reprint rate for plays at this period is higher than that for printed books as a whole, since this process selects for printing only the most popular plays. The publication of *Titus Andronicus* in 1594 fits this pattern and might enable us to fill in some important details of Shakespeare's early career.

In January and February 1594, with the Earl of Sussex's Men playing at the Rose, Henslowe records three performances of a play he renders as 'Titus & ondronicus', which brought him well over £7. The first of these is marked 'ne', but as we have seen, this does not mean that it was new; it is just as likely to signify that it was newly licensed because it had been revised.

Titus is extremely gory. Rape and murder take place on stage; hands and heads are chopped off. The Quarto of *Titus*, however, lacks the celebrated fly-killing scene (3.2), which was printed in the Folio, and which is more powerfully disturbing than the bloodiness elsewhere in the play, since it shows the mental disintegration that results from Titus's and his daughter Lavinia's physical dismemberment. It is likely that this scene was added as part of a revision for the Sussex Men's 1594 season of a play written some years earlier. This was why it needed re-licensing. Presumably, the newly revised and relicensed copy of the play freed up the old allowed copy to be sent to the printer, which is why the scene does not appear in the Quarto.

The right to publish *Titus Andronicus* was entered in the Stationers' Register on 6 February, the day of the third performance of the play by Sussex's Men at the Rose. Its title page does not name the author. Instead, it whets the reader's appetite by advertising its success in performance. It has been played by not one but three theatre companies successively, belonging to the earls of Derby (the title to which Strange had recently succeeded) and Pembroke, as well as Sussex.

It is thought that the short-lived Pembroke's Men, for whom there are records of performances in various towns in southern England in 1592–3, was formed as an offshoot of the amalgamation between Strange's and the Admiral's, allowing the surplus actors to go on a provincial tour. But Henslowe wrote to Alleyn that this tour had been abandoned and the actors had returned to London, forced to 'pawn their apparel'. It seems that one or more individual actors also sought to recoup their costs by selling a short and inaccurate version of the play we know as Shakespeare's *Henry VI* part two for publication as *The Contention of York and Lancaster*.

By April 1594, Lord Strange, Earl of Derby was dead. The result was the disbanding of his acting company, and the transfer of its leading actors to the patronage of the Lord Chamberlain. Shakespeare was probably one of its sharers from the start. He certainly was so by the following Easter, when he is listed as one of the payees for the company's performances at court during the intervening Christmas period. The company was his theatrical home for the rest of his life.

Then in June 1594, Henslowe records the Chamberlain's Men performing together with the Admiral's Men in more Shakespearean-sounding titles. None of these brought him more than a few shillings, perhaps because, as he notes, they were playing out of town at Newington Butts rather than at the Rose. This season included two performances of what he now spells as '*Andronicous*', and one each of *Hamlet* and a play he calls *The Taming of a Shrew*; the Folio title is *The Taming of the Shrew*. We cannot say with certainty that any of these plays individually was by Shakespeare. It is the combination of so many likely sounding titles that is suggestive.

Also in 1594, the Queen's Men published a *Taming of a Shrew* play. It has a similar structure to Shakespeare's, but is set in Athens rather than Padua, and includes a number of quotations from other plays, including some by Marlowe. These actors had previously, in 1591, published *The Troublesome Reign of King John*, which has a plot identical to Shakespeare's *King John* but is written in imitation of Marlowe's *Tamburlaine* and, in contrast to Shakespeare's play, has a sectarian, anti-Catholic ethos. Critics are divided as to whether these versions or Shakespeare's came first, but they fit the story I am telling in this chapter, both as imitations of Shakespeare's theatrical success, and as attempts to correct his perceived literary faults.

For many years, there were critics who wanted to remove *Titus Andronicus* from the Shakespearean canon, feeling it to be too horrible to be by 'gentle' Shakespeare, or too stilted in its language, or with too many abstruse classical allusions, particularly in the first act and parts of the second. The language in these sections certainly sounds different from that of the rest of the play. In these two acts, characters regularly address each other by name, frequently with strings of redundant epithets; they often refer to themselves in the third person; and there is excessive repetition of the same phrase or grammatical construction, both from line to line and from speech to speech. Both in its reference to particular classical practices, and the use of rare words such as 'palliament' (ceremonial gown, 1.1.182), there is a sense of a writer trying primarily to give an impression of Romanness rather than creating individual characterisation. Again, recent statistical work, this time by Brian Vickers, has given new life to the old suggestion that the language in these scenes is more like the work of George Peele than it is like Shakespeare. And yet, even in its first scene, *Titus*, like *1 Henry VI*, makes full use of the stage and its different levels, and is a *tour de force* of plotting.

Thus in both *1 Henry VI* and *Titus* we have the possibility that a play conceived and plotted by Shakespeare, and later attributed to him by his colleagues, includes significant sections that were farmed out to be written by others. The implication of the performance and printing history of these early plays is not only that Shakespeare had had experience as a writer with Queen's, Strange's/Derby's, Pembroke's, and Sussex's Men before becoming a full sharer in the Chamberlain's, but that he was also canny enough to retain ownership of his work, taking it with him from one company to the next. Taken together, it all suggests entrepreneurialism: acting as agent, plotter, and manager, as well as writer, buying material from other authors to complete his project. Perhaps he used his ownership of these and other plays as part capital for his 'share' in the Chamberlain's, and perhaps this financial advantage is the reason for Nash's and 'Greene's' jealousy of him. Far from having only just begun, he was already highly successful, both artistically and commercially, when they made their attacks on him.

1589–94: the Martin Marprelate controversy

The satirical pamphlets by Nash and 'Greene' I have discussed should perhaps be regarded as the fag-end of a controversy that had started a few years earlier. The so-called Marprelate controversy drew in a number of writers and several theatre companies.

It all began with the publication of a lengthy tome entitled *Defence of the Government of the Church of England* (1587) by Dr John Bridges, Dean of Salisbury, which set out to demonstrate that the system of bishops of the Elizabethan English church was grounded in scripture. More extreme Protestants or Presbyterians believed, by contrast, that each individual could speak directly to God, without the need for intercession by priests and the hierarchy of prelates or bishops. Bridges lambasts his Presbyterian opponents for their 'errors' while calling them 'brethren' throughout because they too condemn the 'errors, idolatrie and superstitions' of the papists. A couple of scholarly Presbyterian answers to Bridges were followed in 1588 by a ribald and entertaining pamphlet published by a secret press and written by one calling himself 'Martin Mar-prelate' entitled *Oh Read Over Dr Bridges* or the *Second Epistle to the Terrible Priests*.

What had been somewhat dry theological debate now became popular entertainment, with the government initially (and unadvisedly) encouraging writers to respond in kind. In a collection of epigrams, probably by Thomas Nash and John Lyly, playwright for the St Paul's boys company, we are told that Martin's rustic persona is borrowed from Richard Tarlton (again). But Nash, who wrote a number of pamphlets on the anti-Martinist side, also occasionally did so in the persona of Martin himself. Conveniently, he uses Martin's voice to complain that actors get paid for the 'two hours' of each performance: 'I perceive that every stage player, if he play the fool but two hours together, hath somewhat for his labour' (*Martins Months Minde*, 1589). The controversy soon got out of hand with the result that the children's companies were suppressed entirely. The Queen's Men also fell out of favour at court, perhaps for this reason, and perhaps because of Tarlton's death, although they continued to tour.

Case study: *The Comedy of Errors*

Shakespeare's style does not lend itself to partisan scurrility, and his contribution to this cultural moment may have been something rather different – provided we can accept that an allusion in *The Comedy of Errors* to France 'armed and reverted, making war against her heir' would only have made complete sense between the early spring and late summer of 1589. In the spring, Henri III, King of France, had enlisted the help of the Protestant Henri of Navarre in his ongoing wars against the Catholic League, and in return, officially recognised him as his heir. On 1 August, Henri III was assassinated. Continuing war prevented the coronation of Navarre as Henri IV, but he was immediately recognised in England as King of France. Thus, although the developing political situation did not completely invalidate the joke, it would probably not occur to anyone to write it after that date.

Shakespeare made his play by combining elements from two plays by the Roman poet Plautus. The story of a pair of lost twins comes from *Menaechmi;* the story of a master and slave being locked out of their house because it is occupied by their doubles is from *Amphitruo*. In Shakespeare's play, a master and his slave arrive in Ephesus where, unbeknown to them, their respective twins (also master and slave) have been living ever since they were lost at sea in childhood. Egeus, father to the master twins, has also just arrived in the town and is under sentence of death as an enemy alien. By introducing a second pair of twins, the play increases exponentially the opportunity for 'error', creating hilarious farce even though its story of family separation and loss remains immensely moving. Giving a child the same name as a lost sibling is a psychologically accurate and well-documented way of coping with grief, and yet it is this that facilitates the play's outrageous comedy.

Shakespeare's play changes Plautus's setting, the city of Epidamnus, to Ephesus, famous in the sixteenth century both for its ancient temple of Diana (goddess of both chastity and child-birth), and for being home to an early Christian community. Shakespeare's Ephesus is noted for its witchcraft and superstition, yet instead of the temple to Diana it has a Christian abbey, presided over by a chaste but married abbess. The play long puzzled critics because of its mixture of elements, and the extra-ordinary number of biblical references in its supposedly pagan setting. There are more than sixty quotations from the homilies, the Book of Common Prayer, and the bible including some striking echoes of St Paul's famous letter to the Ephesians. In that letter, Paul describes the relationship between Christ and the church in terms of the duty that wives, servants, and children owe to husbands, masters, and parents, *and* the responsibility that husbands, masters, and parents owe in return to their depen-dants. The play presents a story where (partly because of the mistakes in identity) that bargain breaks down: masters beat their slaves; husbands neglect their wives; and a wife unwittingly commits adultery with her brother-in-law. Violence and mob rule are unleashed – although the staging and timing of all of this mayhem is immensely funny. In the end, the representatives of temporal and spiritual authority, the duke and the abbess, who turns out to be Egeus's lost wife and mother to one of the sets of twins, unravel the knots, and peace is restored.

This is the only Shakespeare play that both incorporates so many mixed matters of religion, and has a known performance in a context where matters of religion played a significant part. This took place at Gray's Inn very late in the evening on Innocents' Day, 26 December 1594. Gray's is one of the Inns of Court – colleges that provide legal training, and which at that time also functioned as finishing schools for young gentlemen. The performance, given by a professional company of actors, which we can only assume was the Chamberlain's Men, was part of a three-month-long festival of misrule. Later described and published as the *Gesta Grayorum*, this was organised by the students, and designed to demonstrate the Inn's loyalty to the crown, particularly in matters of religion. The festival would culminate in a Shrovetide performance by the students at court, where the queen and 'Britton land' would be praised for being a 'mighty rock', a refuge for 'People oppressed' by 'tempests' abroad – a clear reference to the fact that so many Protestant refugees from persecution in Spain and France had found a home in England. Shakespeare's play and the *Gesta* share a good deal of language and imagery, particularly regarding the danger of superstition, which suggests that some script conferencing had taken place between the students and the actors. If *The Comedy of Errors* was originally written in 1589, the text that has come down to us may therefore have been a revision made for that performance at Gray's Inn. Perhaps significantly, Dr Bridges (the person whose book sparked the Marprelate controversy) had been admitted to the Inn as an honorary member only nine months previously.

The students who were responsible for arranging the festivities wrote to all members of the Inn requesting their support. The queen's chief minister, William Cecil, a former student, had responded generously; it is possible he would have wanted to keep an eye on what these young gentlemen were up to. A few years earlier the Privy Council had had occasion to send a warning letter to the masters at Gray's accusing them of harbouring Roman Catholic priests and allowing the celebration of mass. Having the Chamberlain's Men perform at court the play they would take to Gray's would be one way of doing that, and it may therefore be this play for which Shakespeare and his fellows received payment for a court performance that Christmas, also on Innocents' Day but presumably earlier in the day.

SHAKESPEARE'S LIFE AND WORKS: DOCUMENTED EVENTS

1564	William Shakespeare baptised in Stratford parish church, 26 April.
1576	James Burbage erects the Theatre, the first purpose-built theatre in England.
1582	Special marriage licence granted for the marriage of William Shakespeare and Anne Hathaway, with accompanying marriage bond, 27 and 28 November.
1583	Shakespeare's daughter Susanna christened in Stratford, 26 May.
1585	The twins Judith and Hamnet christened in Stratford, 2 February.
1592	Philip Henslowe, owner of the Rose Theatre, records sixteen (or seventeen) performances there of *Harey the VI* by Lord Strange's Men.
	Reference to Alleyn as Talbot in Nash's *Pierce Penniless*.
	Attack on Shake-scene in *Greene's Groatsworth of Wit*.
1592–4	London theatres closed by plague: July–December 1592; Februrary–December 1593; and Februrary–March 1594.
1593	*Venus and Adonis* published; a prefatory letter addressed to the Earl of Southampton requests his patronage. The right to publish was entered on 18 April by the printer Richard Field, also from Stratford.

SHAKESPEARE'S LIFE AND WORKS: DOCUMENTED EVENTS (*cont.*)

1594	Henslowe records three performances of *Titus & ondronicus* by Sussex's Men at the Rose on 28 January, and two of *Andronicous* and of *The Taming of A Shrew* by the Admiral's and Chamberlain's Men at his theatre in Newington in June. The right to publish *Titus* was entered in the Stationers' Register on 6 February.
	Publication of *The Rape of Lucrece*, confidently dedicated to Southampton, entered 9 May, with eight editions before 1640.
	Performance of *The Comedy of Errors* at Gray's Inn, 26 December.
1595	Chamber accounts, 15 March: Shakespeare and other sharers in the Chamberlain's Men are paid for two performances at court the previous Christmas, on 26 and 28 December.
1596	Grant of arms to John Shakespeare, 20 October.
1597	William Shakespeare purchases New Place, Stratford, 4 May.
1598–9	The Theatre is dismantled and rebuilt on Bankside as the Globe. Shakespeare becomes a sharer in the building.
1603	Letters Patent granted to Shakespeare and his fellow sharers by James I. They become His Majesties Servants, or the King's Men, May.
1609 and 1610	The public theatres were closed for much of the time because of plague. The King's Men are paid for rehearsal time to prepare them for the two Christmas performance seasons at court.
1616	Shakespeare buried in Holy Trinity, Stratford, 25 April.
1623	Publication of the First Folio collection of Shakespeare's plays.

The performance at Gray's was intended to function as part of a staged breakdown in relations between the Inn and its neighbour, the Inner Temple, which would then be smoothed over in a show of 'Amity' a few days later. Maybe this was another reason why the play was chosen. It is notable for its rejection of extremes, for its toleration, and the clemency shown at the end by the duke. Rather than reinforcing division, it celebrates difference. It ends not with the twin masters but with the twin slaves. And it movingly suggests that identical twins, and by implication things that look the same (as the various branches of Christianity each claimed to be the one true, prior, and original religion), may in fact have different identities and should allow each other to go in parallel:

> We came into the world like brother and brother
> And now lets go hand in hand, not one before another.

The play is quintessential Shakespeare: a brilliantly funny romp in situation, language, and use of the stage; a deftly managed plot; and as a result, a complex, enduring set of ethical questions.

3
Shakespeare's structures: plot, genre, and character

How may likeness, made in crimes,
Make a practice on the times.

(Measure for Measure, 3.2.255–6)

Shakespeare has always been celebrated for the qualities of his language, but the last chapter argued that his financial and artistic success in the theatre may have been largely due to the fact that he was also particularly skilled as a *plotter* of plays. The idea that someone who writes plays should be 'more the poet of his plots than of his verses' is one of the most important perceptions in the *Poetics* – the world's most influential treatise on the writing of tragedy, by the ancient Greek philosopher Aristotle. Nevertheless, plotting is rarely considered by literary critics of drama, and is entirely absent from many introductions to Shakespeare.

This is probably because the word 'plot' is often used interchangeably with 'story'. Film critics, however, always and rightly insist on the distinction between story and plot: the story consists of a series of events of cause and effect in chronological order; the plot is the *arrangement* of those events so that they intrigue and draw in an audience. Thus the Latin poet Horace in his *Art of Poetry* recommended that one should always begin a story 'in the middle'. And French film-maker François

Truffaut, asked whether his films had a beginning, a middle, and an end, famously replied that yes they did, but not necessarily in that order.

The term 'maker' was also used to describe poets and dramatists during the sixteenth century, although a dramatist who wanted to appear gentlemanly might insist on the word 'poet' – not unreasonably, since many sixteenth-century plays, particularly tragedies, are written in verse. The word 'playwright', however, seems to have been invented as a term of abuse. Note the spelling of that word: not 'play-write', but a word like wheelwright or shipwright, someone who puts plays together; a lower-class maker or craftsman. It lends itself to being combined with the adjective 'common' – as in the derogatory phrase 'common player' to signify 'actor'. It first occurs in a sonnet by one who calls himself 'Cygnus' (Swan) found amongst several commendatory poems by different writers that preface Ben Jonson's *Sejanus* (1605). Writers should be 'masters of their art' says Cygnus; and it is through his wit, and his ability to retrieve a vivid sense of the past, that Jonson has shown 'The crew / Of common play-wrights' how to do it.

The distinction 'Cygnus' is making is between 'writing well' and cobbling things together – slinging in the crowd-pleasing aspects that sold well last time, perhaps, or lifting phrases directly from other writers without much thought as to how to integrate the ideas. Since the published text of *Sejanus* is full of precise references to classical sources, Cygnus is not saying that a writer should not borrow his material, but rather that he should use it with judgement, finesse, and wit, transforming it into something that is unique to him. That is where his originality lies. It is the way that the material is used that creates the individual voice of the poet – and the plot.

Shakespeare's way of writing well, like Jonson's, also embodies wit, taken to extremes in his exuberant love of puns. But Shakespeare also matches this flexibility, or multi-valency of

words with multi-valent plots. He constructs a play by borrow-
ing stories from a variety of different sources and combining
them in a single plot so that they bounce off each other, reflect-
ing and refracting, creating a rich context of similarity and difference. This allows readers and audiences to gain multiple
perspectives on the problem encompassed by the central story.
And it is this that makes the plays infinitely reinterpretable.

It seems that Jonson recognised this when he came to write
his eulogy on Shakespeare – whom he calls 'sweet swan of
Avon' – which is printed amongst the commendatory verses at
the beginning of the 1623 First Folio. While most of the poem
is devoted to Shakespeare's language, Jonson also distinguishes
between 'designs' (the plot) and the 'dressing of his lines' (the
poetry), while the lines themselves are not just written, but
constructed, or 'made': 'so richly spun, and woven so fit'.
Though he begins his poem addressing Shakespeare the poet as
'spirit of the age' it is this consideration of verse *plus* design and
construction that culminates in this poem's more famous observation, 'He was not for an age, but for all time!'

Putting a plot together – case study: *King Lear*

When asked to tell the story of *King Lear*, most people will begin
with something like: 'Lear is an old man with three daughters.
He has decided to divide his kingdom between them, and asks
each of them to say which of them loves him best.' This is
perfectly correct in terms of Lear's story, but it is not where
Shakespeare has chosen to start his play. Instead, a character
named Gloucester in the text, but whose name we do not know
if we are watching the play, tells us and his companion briefly
about the division of the kingdom in terms of Lear's preferences
for one or other of his two sons-in-law. Then, in response to the

first speaker's next question, he talks about his relationship with his own two sons.

If we were watching the play we would gain an immense amount of information almost before the characters began to speak. Here are two older men, well-dressed, authoritative in their manner, and of equal status. They belong in this court. We may not know their names, but they clearly know each other, though they may not have met for some time; perhaps the first speaker has been away, which is why he is asking for confirmation of what is happening.

When asked about the third person, a young man, who is standing with them, the second speaker begins a series of jokes about the expense ('Charge') of bringing him up, which puns on the charge (accusation) that he is the young man's father. Although he never quite says as much, it is clear what he means: the young man is illegitimate. But the questioner, perhaps a little embarrassed that the father is talking about the young man in this way, replies, 'I cannot conceive you'. This is the cue for the father to joke about the 'sport' he had with the young man's unmarried mother and how she had conceived. He then says he has an older son and loves them both equally. But for the last nine years, the young man has been brought up in another family (as was common in medieval and early modern England), and he is about to be sent away again. The young man, now named Edmund, is polite, indeed silent, until introduced by his father to his friend, now identified as the Duke of Kent.

The father's lack of concern about his son's feelings in this short scene has told us a great deal about family relationships in this society. Kent, however, has made a couple of attempts to stop or deflect him. It is a signal that we do not have to dismiss the father's ribald, unkind, unthinking behaviour as just something they did 'back then' (whether in ancient Britain, where the story is set, or in Shakespeare's England). If Kent is embarrassed by it, so can we be.

The next time we see Edmund, he is seething with anger at the injustice of his position as 'bastard'. And having seen and heard his father joking about his mother in front of his face, we might well understand why. The first scene has thus set up the plot of the play, its theme of parental irresponsibility and the game-playing that passes for family life in dysfunctional families, which too often results in the scapegoating of children – identifying the child as the problem rather than the poisonous family dynamic. In just a few minutes Cordelia, Lear's 'good' daughter, will similarly be cast as problem child when she refuses to play the game that Lear has set up.

Elements of Shakespeare's *Lear* plot

The Gloucester family story is therefore an essential part of the plot of *King Lear*, not a 'subplot'. It functions as a touchstone whereby we can better understand the issues raised by the Lear family story. It provides us with a toe-curlingly accurate portrayal of the way parents often talk about their children in front of them. It is a depressingly ordinary, familiar, realistic scenario. The Lear story is very familiar too, but this time from fairy tale – three daughters, a love test, two wicked sisters. In its specific form as a story about a king of ancient Britain, it is found in Holinshed's *Chronicle* (1577) and also in the *Mirror for Magistrates* (1559), one of a series of cautionary tragic tales illustrating, among other things, the dangers of despotic government, and the perils of dividing up a country. It is usually found with a happy ending in which Lear ends his days with his youngest daughter, and with an overt moral message about obedience to authority. In this form, it also appears as the storyline for the old play *King Leir*, which we have seen was in the Queen's Men's repertoire when they performed at Henslowe's Rose Theatre in the early 1590s. It is this version of the story that is retold in a moral ballad which was popular and often reprinted through the seventeenth century.

Despite the realism with which he invests the opening, Shakespeare had found the material for the Gloucester family part of his plot in Sir Philip Sydney's pastoral prose epic, *Arcadia*. There, in the middle of a storm, the princes Pyrocles and Musidorus come across an old blind man being led by his son, Leonatus. The old man, once king of Paphlagonia, tells them he was fooled by his concubine into both giving command of his kingdom to his illegitimate son, Plexirtus, and agreeing to have Leonatus murdered. Fortunately the murderers took pity on Leonatus and let him go. Plexirtus, however, became tyrannous and, not content with ruling the kingdom, also wanted the name of king. He therefore put out his father's eyes and cast him out, forbidding anyone to help him. Leonatus, who had been living as a poor man, came to his aid, only disobeying his father in refusing to take him to a rock where he might commit suicide. Eventually, Plexirtus is beaten, the old man crowns Leonatus as king, and dies, 'his heart broken with unkindness and affliction, stretched so far beyond his limits with this excess of comfort, as it was able no longer to keep safe his royal spirits'.

This story furnishes Shakespeare with a number of ideas for Gloucester's role in the play: his illegitimate son, Edmund; his blinding by the duke of Cornwall; and the iconic scene in which his true son Edgar, first disguised as the madman and beggar Poor Tom, leads him to what he describes as Dover cliff and then, having assumed a peasant's accent, tries to persuade him that he has indeed fallen from the top of the cliff onto the beach below. It also supplies the concept and some of the words for the deaths of both Gloucester and Lear – the heart being stretched or racked with misery and breaking in blessed release. Edgar tells us that when Gloucester recognised him as his true son, his heart 'burst smilingly'(5.3.199); later as he tries to pull Lear back from the brink of death, Kent stops him:

Vex not his ghost. O let him pass. He hates him
That would upon the rack of this tough world
Stretch him out longer.

(5.3.313–15)

In the Folio version of this scene, Kent suggests it is better for
Lear to die thinking Cordelia is still alive. The play thus
curiously preserves, for Lear himself, the happy ending found in
most of the sources and the ballads. It does this while intensify-
ing the sense of tragedy and loss for us.

The transformation of the fairy tale, Cinderella-like material
into the plot that is Shakespeare's *King Lear* depends on its inclusion of the Gloucester family story. But the story Shakespeare
found in the *Arcadia* was told in retrospect from the point of
view of the two characters who are met by the young princes
(and by us) at the end of their story; the blinded man being led
by his faithful son is an extraordinary image, in a romance
convention. This time, by showing the story from its negligible
beginnings in family banter, Shakespeare renders it ordinary,
despite the aristocratic status of the characters. It thereby trian-
gulates with the story of Lear and his daughters, *and* with the
story that many of us might tell about ourselves and our parents,
our siblings, or our children, and creates space for a hugely
enriched, more complex response to the ostensible subject
matter, Lear.

Tyrannies never burst fully formed into the world. They
begin small, often in response to some real or perceived injustice. The everyday domesticity of Gloucester's attitude to his
family provides that small beginning. It gives an explanation for
Edmund's later cruelty, although it is not an excuse. We cannot
continue to blame our parents for the bad things that happen to
us or that we do to others. But the perspective provided by this
glimpse of his upbringing makes him humanly believable, and
not a monster. This extends too to Lear's daughters. Productions

that too obviously costume and present the daughters in the first scene as two wicked sisters and one innocent heroine are playing the end of the play before the beginning, and render Lear's actions stupid. Goneril and Regan do not set out to kill their father and create a civil war, they merely want their inheritance while they are young enough to enjoy it. Richard Eyre's production at the National Theatre (1997) introduced a telling touch in the scene which shows family life when Lear and his hundred knights are living in Goneril's castle (1.4). As they left the stage after their raucous and disruptive return from hunting, she flicked a small piece of mud off her nice white table-cloth. She clearly found them intolerable – with some justification.

Later in the play when things have gone too far, her husband, Albany, calls her a monster. Nice man though he may be, he has taken a back seat throughout; he has watched the mounting injustices but done nothing to intervene. It is not enough simply to accuse her of monstrousness when his neglect has allowed that monstrousness to flourish. Thus, what started out in the sources as the moral injunction of chronicle history on the one hand, and moral romance on the other, becomes what many critics have seen as one of the bleakest and most psychologically compelling plays in the canon.

Patterns of folly

In the brutal society which Lear's actions have, in part, created, anyone who speaks out against injustice is colloquially speaking 'mad', as is anyone who stays with him, or joins him, once he becomes ostracised. Lear's own developing mental breakdown is therefore played out against a succession of foolish or mad advisers and helpers. First the Fool himself, the only person in Lear's household who can satirise the folly and corruption of his court with impunity because he dresses it up in witty sayings and songs; next Kent, his faithful servant, banished like Cordelia for speaking his mind, but who returns as the blunt-speaking Caius; and finally Edgar, who in his disguise as the madman Poor Tom crosses between the Gloucester and Lear family stories and helps tie them together.

As Lear becomes mad, so he leaves behind his faithful but worldly wise and satirical Fool and turns to the sympathetic Poor Tom, whom he has welcomed as a representative of naked humanity, a reminder that he had 'taken / Too little care of this', and therefore as his 'philosopher' (3.4.32–3; 150). This progression of folly to madness and then a kind of wisdom is perhaps why the Fool can disappear in the middle. Once Lear has gone mad, and is paradoxically beginning to 'see better', his own language incorporates some of the satirical social commentary previously voiced by the Fool:

> What, art mad? A man may see how this world goes with no eyes. Look with thine ears. See how yond justice rails upon yond simple thief. Hark in thine ear; change places and which is the justice, which is the thief?
>
> (4.6.150–4)

When the king can say this, the Fool no longer has a function.

The transition is clearer in the Folio version of the play, particularly in changes made to the earlier hovel scene, where all the designated mad or foolish characters take refuge from the storm. The Quarto version of this scene contains a good deal of 'mad' language for Tom as he pretends to see devils, which is borrowed from Scott's *Discovery of Witchcraft*. There is also a mock trial of Goneril; Lear requires Tom and the Fool to sit on the bench beside him as justices, while a stool is made to stand in for his daughter. Both these elements are a *tour de force* of writing. They are memorable and entertaining, but they arguably detract from the overall shape of the play, lose the idea that Lear is growing away from the Fool, and disturbingly provoke unquestioning audience laughter for what is a grotesque travesty of justice. The Folio revision of this scene cuts them.

Instead, in response to Lear's retreat into madness and sleep, 'We'll go to supper i' the' morning', the Folio adds a half line for the Fool: 'And I'll go to bed at noon' (3.6.84–5). It is the point where he gives up, and a number of late twentieth-century productions had him lie down next to Lear at this point and then die. But this rather sentimental solution would not be practical on an Elizabethan stage, where without the benefit of a blackout, dead bodies have to be carried off. The Fool has stayed with Lear faithfully, braving the discomfort of the heath and the storm. As Lear's household servant he is entitled to be given board and lodging; but in this world turned upside down, that bargain of his employment has been denied him. Although he is given a function at the end of the scene as it appears in the Quarto, he is not needed in the remainder of the Folio's version. All this suggests that the Folio expects him to go on his way here, perhaps to seek another household somewhere else where his talents would be appreciated, thus creating a sense of a world elsewhere, that goes on untouched by the tragedy. The extra Folio line makes a perfect exit. No exit stage direction is marked in the text but missing stage directions are not unusual in printed plays of this period.

This great tragedy is made more bleakly devastating by the Fool's worldly satire, and by the fleeting promises afforded by those moments that owe more to renaissance artifice and classical ideas of divinely inspired madness than they do to reality in any age. But Shakespeare's tragic structure needs to transmute the comedy. It must get rid of the Fool to concentrate on Lear's foolish fond old man. The next time we see Lear will be where barren heath gives way to gentler countryside and then flowering cornfields, and where, in the tradition of renaissance pastoral, he loses his wits but finds himself. It is a triumphant example of the kind of 'tragical-comical-historical-pastoral' play that, in *Hamlet*, Polonius disparagingly says is offered by the theatre troupe that visits Elsinore.

HISTORY AND TRAGEDY – EXPERIMENTS IN FORM

The term 'tragedy' was still relatively unknown and fluid when Shakespeare began writing, although it seems it had first been brought into English by Chaucer in *The Canterbury Tales* as a description of the Monk's Tale. It was used in a similar vein to describe some of the warning tales of misrule and corruption collected in *The Mirror for Magistrates* (1559). Tragedy as demonstrated in these works is an exploration of the turning of fortune's wheel, the vanity of human wishes, the transience of human life and of worldly success. It is epitomised in the five-act drama *Gorboduc*, the first designated tragic play to be written in English (1561), in which King Gorboduc divides Britain between his two sons. But just as classical tragedies took the well-known stories of Greek myth and history, so *Gorboduc* spawned a new genre of English history play, made popular by Robert Greene, Christopher Marlowe, George Peele, and of course Shakespeare. The words 'history' and 'tragedy' are therefore often interchangeable in the titles of some of these plays. The Quarto of *King Lear,* for example, appeared as the *True Chronicle History of the Life and Death of King Lear,* and the 1604 *Hamlet* as *The Tragical History of Hamlet, Prince of Denmark.*

Shakespeare's mixed genre

The plays of Shakespeare collected in the 1623 Folio, printed seven years after his death, are divided into three sections, corresponding to the full title of that book: *Mr William*

Shakespeare's Comedies, Histories, and Tragedies. But individual plays invariably contain both 'low' and 'high' characters, as well as coarse and elevated language, and even the two distinct genres of comedy and tragedy. There are jokes in all the tragedies, and the comedies all begin in dangerous conflict; most of the mature comedies even end with significant discordant undertones. In short, Shakespeare's plays mix genres and break the rules.

From the very beginning, this has led other writers to point to his lack of a university education and assume that if he was tutored at all, it was by natural genius – in Milton's words from his poem 'L'Allegro', 'Sweetest Shakespeare, fancy's child,/Warble his native woodnotes wild'. It became common-place to praise Shakespeare for the beauties of his poetry, while deploring his ignorance of play construction as set out by classical authors. Nahum Tate's preface to the printed edition of his version of *King Lear* (1681), for instance, praises Shakespeare's 'images and language' as 'so odd and surprising, and yet so agreeable and proper, that ... we are satisfied that they were the only things in the world that ought to be said on those occasions'. But he finds them 'a heap of jewels, unstrung and unpolished; yet so dazzling in their disorder, that I soon perceived I had seized a treasure'. Reordering and streamlining this treasure involved starting the play with Edmund announcing his ambition, and substituting a love story between Cordelia and Edgar for that between Cordelia and the King of France. He adds frisson by having Edgar in disguise save Cordelia, also in disguise, from near rape by Edmund's 'ruffians', and ends the play with Edgar rescuing Cordelia and Lear from prison in the nick of time. The result is rather sentimental: true love wins out against bastardy and baseness.

Popular entertainment, whether Victorian novel, Elizabethan play, or Hollywood movie, tends to give tidy endings to stories that in life would be messy and provisional. A

GENRE

In modern usage the term 'genre fiction' tends to describe, for example, different types of crime story; the detective story, the thriller, the police drama each have strict conventions for character, setting, and language. Classical Greek drama recognised three different forms of play: tragedy, comedy, and the satyr play, which was performed during play competitions as an afterpiece. This was perhaps a satirical commentary on what had gone before, although we are not very sure about this because only one example has come down to us: *Cyclops* by Euripides. Classical drama has very tight and demanding structures: events generally occur in one geographical space over a short length of time, and violence takes place off stage. Characters in tragedies are gods and high-class mortals; they speak in an elevated style and do not make jokes. Characters in comedies, by contrast, are citizens and slaves.

The standard ideas about tragedy are set out in the *Poetics* by the ancient Greek philosopher Aristotle and seemed immutable to critics in the Renaissance. The Roman poet Horace in his *Art of Poetry* tentatively allowed for the possibility that satyr plays might mix tragedy and comedy conventions, but his comments on the subject are ambivalent and unclear. The only known Latin mixed genre play is *Amphitruo* by Plautus, written about a hundred years before Horace, and used by Shakespeare as a source for both *The Taming of the Shrew* and *The Comedy of Errors*. It has a prologue in which Mercury, messenger of the gods, explains, half defiantly and half humorously, that it is a *'tragicocomedia'* (literally 'tragedy with comedy') because, although it concerns one of Jupiter's many adulteries, 'it has a slave in it'.

It is erroneously stated in many literary histories that tragicomedy was introduced into England by John Fletcher in *The Faithful Shepherdess* (c. 1608, based on Guarini's *Il Pastor Fido*, written in the early 1580s). In fact the first designated 'tragical comedy' in England was Richard Edwards's *Damon and Pythias* (1564, printed 1571 and 1581), a play about good governance and the reform of a noted tyrant.

play or film must not only stop but must stop at a point when we feel that everything necessary has been said: the lovers are reunited, or alternatively, the protagonists are dead before our eyes while some lesser figure sums up and arranges the future government of the kingdom. But perhaps one of the reasons why Shakespeare's plays remain fresh and reinterpretable is that his language and structures undercut those certainties. Perhaps he learnt this technique from his experience of writing history plays, which by definition are snapshots in an unending series of events that a commercially minded playwright may want to explore further in the future. In these circumstances, closure is neither historically possible nor financially desirable. As everyone watching knows, France so gloriously won in one play will be lost again in the next. Come and buy a ticket.

It is often said that our sense of genre depends on where the play stops. *King Lear* has a happy ending, but this occurs at the end of Act IV when Lear and his daughter Cordelia are reunited; there is still an act to go. But the song that the Fool sings earlier on in that play with the refrain 'The rain it raineth every day' had already been used by Shakespeare once before, as the elegiac coda to *Twelfth Night.* This play, usually regarded as one of the happiest of Shakespeare's so-called happy comedies only turns out well in its very last moments; even in the final scene the heroine, Viola, is threatened with death by Orsino, the man she loves, while the very much wronged but kill-joy household steward, Malvolio, is so humiliated that he leaves the stage threatening: 'I'll be revenged on the whole pack of you' (5.1.364). This play has had moments that teeter on the edge of tragedy from its opening scene, where Orsino is sick almost unto death for love for Olivia; to the next scene in which Viola is desperate about the presumed loss of her brother in a shipwreck; to the scene where Olivia excessively mourns a dead brother; to the one in which Viola, in disguise, manfully woos her on behalf of the man she loves.

Clearly the division into comedies, histories, and tragedies does not work very well for Shakespeare's plays. A number of other categories have therefore been introduced in attempts to overcome this difficulty. The term 'romance' is often used to account for the fantastical worlds encountered in *The Tempest, The Winter's Tale*, and *Cymbeline*, which was included amongst the tragedies in the Folio. Sometimes all three get grouped as 'late plays', or 'last plays', and then compared with Beethoven's 'late quartets', as the insights of a great writer at the end of his life – although since Shakespeare was only fifty-two when he died, this seems premature. Increasingly *The Winter's Tale* and *Cymbeline* are now termed tragicomedies, although usually with a pastoral romance, rather than a political, understanding of that term (see text box, p. 85). For much of the twentieth century, *All's Well that Ends Well, Measure for Measure, Troilus and Cressida*, and even *Hamlet* were considered 'problem plays', a term coined by the critic F.S. Boas, inspired by Ibsen's plays about social and sexual issues. But this is a category with huge problems of definition. All good plays are problem plays, or at least plays about a problem.

None of these genre distinctions are particularly helpful, and some have been distinctly misleading, since readers' expectations of genre will encourage them to read in certain ways, and they may therefore resist the notion that the great tragedies can in places be funny, or the 'happy', 'festive' comedies sad. It seems better to accept that Shakespeare's plays are simply plays, which mix any or all of the elements of drama as necessary, according to the way he wishes to present or plot his mingled stories. Shakespeare forbears easy answers and definite closure, thus preserving the problems his plays all undoubtedly contain for the audience to wonder about.

It is, for example, instructive to chart his treatment of death in a tragedy like *Macbeth*. We tend to think of death as uniformly sad or horrible but this play presents it in a variety of ways that shape audience understanding and reception of the story, and complicate our response. The first significant death takes place in the past and off stage on a distant battlefield; a captain, covered in blood from his own wounds, tells King Duncan about Macbeth's victory, saying that he has 'unseamed' his enemy 'from the nave to the chaps'. This appallingly brutal injury will have spilt the man's guts. The bloodied captain has expressed it as the neat unpicking of a garment – although with a terrible pun on unseamed, since the wound will have made the man quite unlike himself. The battlefield, covered in dead bodies, is iconic; he says it recalls Golgotha, the site of Christ's crucifixion, which itself means 'place of the skull' – the grave of Adam, the first man in the biblical creation story. The bloodshed, present before our eyes in the exhausted, bloodstained captain, is thus disguised, rendering Macbeth's actions archetypal and heroic (1.2.7–45).

The next death is of Duncan himself while he is a guest in Macbeth's castle. This murder sins against loyalty to the king, as well as the law of hospitality, but a succession of scenes (1.7–2.2) concentrate on the state of mind of the murderers. Macbeth is apprehensive; he hallucinates an air-drawn dagger, which compels him on his way (2.1.33). Lady Macbeth hears or thinks she hears a sound – an owl shriek, perhaps (2.2.2–3) – and imagines him going into the king's chamber; she has drugged the grooms so they will hear nothing. Then, after the murder, he returns to the stage, the bloody daggers now in his hand. The hero of the battle-field is dismayed; the grooms were woken by a dream of murder, and had called on God before going back to sleep; Macbeth thinks he has heard a voice cry repeatedly 'sleep no more'. His wife busily takes charge, but she reveals that she would have happily done the deed if Duncan had not looked like her father as he slept. It is the Macbeths' banal human fears that come through in these scenes, and the petty sordidness of their crime. But we are with them throughout the process, seeing and hearing partly through their senses, as they both screw their courage to the sticking place (cf. 1.7.60). We are therefore inevitably on their side, sharing their anxiety. When Macduff arrives the following morning and discovers the dead body, the description he gives is of the 'sacrilegious' desecration of the 'Lord's anointed temple' (2.3.65–6). Shortly afterwards, when Macduff challenges Macbeth on why he has killed the grooms, Macbeth picks up on this otherworldly idea of Duncan's death, 'his silver skin laced with his golden blood' (2.3.111). It is too grand for our human pity, and we don't yet want the Macbeths to be discovered.

A third murder is meant to remove Banquo and his son Fleance from the succession to the throne. Macbeth's hired thugs lie in wait for them as they travel back to the castle after dark. Banquo is killed before our eyes, but the deed is distanced from Macbeth himself. In the struggle the murderers' lamp goes out and they grope around in the dark. They are no longer so dangerous; they are even comically incompetent, and the child escapes (3.3.19–20). We can be glad.

It is probably not until the fourth set of murders that the audience is finally made to experience the horror of Macbeth's tyranny over Scotland. Lady Macduff is in her castle with her son, abandoned by her husband who has fled to England. Dependable Ross is with her, but tells her he is afraid, admitting 'Cruel are the times when we are traitors and do not know ourselves' (4.2.18); then he leaves. Lady Macduff talks to her son about his father and tells him that he is dead. The boy is precocious and notes that if he were really dead she would weep for him; 'if you would not it were a good sign that I should quickly have a new father'. We laugh, knowingly. A messenger bursts in and tells her to fly, but he is too frightened to stay longer. Macbeth's henchmen enter. One of them announces that Macduff is a traitor; the boy runs at him, attacking him. In one production I saw many years ago the man picked him up and bounced him on his knee, laughing, 'What you egg!' – as you do with a child. Then, suddenly, he stabbed him: 'Young fry of treachery'. The image is of a young fish, the traitor's spawn, but the terrible pun of fried egg is not inappropriate here either. It is a deeply inappropriate, indeed offensive act – the worst possible – and we need to be made to squirm.

In Shakespeare's later plays, such horrors are often preceded or accompanied by the kind of laughter that is triggered by shock, and which, because it is laughter and therefore the 'wrong' reaction, reinforces shock and ends in a gasp. Being the 'wrong' reaction it implicates us too. Even if we did not laugh, we are like the three men who have not dared to stop to protect the mother and child; we too did nothing. Of course not, we're in a theatre. But it is the image of the dead child that is left in our minds at the end of the scene, since Lady Macduff is hustled away to be murdered off stage.

Later in England, Macduff is brought news of the annihilation of his family. He is overwhelmed first into stunned silence and then an outburst in which he blames himself (4.3.207–25). Malcolm, who is with him, first urges him to give sorrow words, but is then embarrassed by his grief and tells him to pull himself together (4.3.220). Now at last we are allowed to see the human cost of what *we* have gone along with throughout the play. The chances are, however, that like Ross and all the others, including Macduff himself, we would go along with it in life too. Indeed, we have just witnessed, at the beginning of that scene, Macduff being prepared to accept any amount of iniquity if only Malcolm would claim the throne. By mixing genres, Shakespeare is able to pace and complicate audience reactions, both drawing us in emotionally – even to the extent of becoming virtual participants in events – and giving us the perspective to reflect critically on them.

Shakespeare and the Aristotelian unities

I suggested above (pp. 35–9) that Shakespeare changed the text of *Hamlet* because he had changed his mind about the idea of 'tragic flaw', considered to be the principle cause of tragedy in Aristotle's *Poetics*. In this chapter I have argued that, like Aristotle, he understood the importance of plot, but unlike Aristotle, rejected the need to keep his plays generically pure. I intend to show that, whether or not he had read the *Poetics,* Shakespeare had a better understanding of what Aristotle meant by 'unity' than those contemporaries who accused him of writing incorrectly.

Aristotle's *Poetics* was not published in England even in Latin translation until after Shakespeare's death, although it was available from European booksellers in Greek, Latin, and Italian throughout the sixteenth century. The Italian renaissance commentators on Aristotle, notably Lodovico Castelvetro (*c.* 1505–71), also widely available, wrongly stated that Aristotle insists that a play should obey the 'three unities' of time, place, and action. In fact, Aristotle stipulates only that a play must have a unity of action, although of course it may appear easier to achieve this ideal if time and place are restricted. Shakespeare always achieves a unity of action, even in those plays that cover great tracts of time and space, or which mix tragedy and comedy; his plots are complex but thoroughly integrated. Shakespeare understood what every playacting child knows, but which educated adults forget, that the rules of a game can allow wildly disparate things to be brought together or to stand in for one another. Provided the *action* is coherent, time and place can look after themselves.

Shakespeare only wrote two plays that abide by the unities of time and place: *The Comedy of Errors* is set in a small town and takes place within a single span of twenty-four hours; *The Tempest* is set on a small island, and takes place almost in real time, between 2pm and 6pm. The plot of *A Midsummer Night's Dream* takes slightly longer than twenty-four hours and moves from Athens to the wood just outside. In all other plays, he does not stint to break the 'rules', sometimes quite markedly. The English history plays of course inevitably cover long periods of historical time, although he disguises that by making the action seem both continuous and shorter, telescoping battles fought over a number of years into one event. In his later plays, however, he is much bolder. *Cymbeline* has characters travelling from Britain to Italy and into the depths of Wales; its Britain is ancient and Celtic, but its Italy seems to veer between classical Rome and the renaissance. *The Winter's Tale*, most daringly of all, brings on the character of Time in the middle of the play to comment directly on the 'crime' of passing over a gap of sixteen years between one scene and the next, although the previous scene has already effected a change of place from Sicily to Bohemia, and a change of mood from tragedy to pastoral comedy. Shakespeare is not just breaking the rules, he is knowingly breaking the rules, and Time's speech (4.1.1–32) constitutes one of the few overt pieces of literary theory that he has left us.

The plot of *Antony and Cleopatra* covers more than twenty years and spans the entire classical world. Scenes are set in Alexandria, Rome, and Greece, pitting the eastern and western parts of the Roman Empire against each other. Its third and fourth act battles switch between the armies in a succession of breathless, short scenes (see text box opposite), some without dialogue – no more than the passage of armed men over the stage. In total, *Antony and Cleopatra* has as many as forty-three scenes with the Battle of Actium numerically as well as dramaturgically occupying the scenes in the very centre (3.7–3.11).

Cleopatra has insisted that this battle should take place at sea; water is her own, changeable medium, and she insists too that she should take part. But at the crucial moment she takes flight, and Antony, tied to her by his heartstrings (cf. 3.11.58), follows her – or, as one of his dismayed followers puts it, shamefully flies after her, 'like a doting mallard' (3.10.20–4). It is the fatal pivotal moment. When John Dryden rewrote the play as *All for Love* (1677), trying to correct its 'faults', he began with Actium and told the earlier history as reminiscence. This does not make it a more exciting play.

ACT AND SCENE CONSTRUCTION

An Elizabethan schoolboy would have been taught that a Latin play was divided into five acts, each act completing a specific conceptual phase in the drama. But act division is not readily apparent to audiences and readers unless it is marked in some way – perhaps by a chorus or a musical interlude. Music was later introduced between acts in the Jacobean private theatres but this was not the practice in the Elizabethan public theatres.

On the bare Elizabethan stage, a change of scene occurs when one set of characters leaves the stage empty and is replaced by a different set. Depending on the identity of the new characters, the props they carry, and/or the words they say, this may also imply a change of time and location. This kind of scene change is readily apparent to audiences and also to readers.

Although Elizabethan dramatists may have conceived their plays in acts, and certainly used scene division structurally as a way of presenting the story, few early playtexts formally mark these divisions. No Shakespearean quarto, with the exception of *Othello* (printed 1622), makes act divisions, although even this lacks the division for Act 3. Of the thirty-seven plays in the Folio, ten mark act divisions only, and a further nineteen number acts and scenes. The remainder, though evidently written in scenes, are unmarked except for an initial Latin *'Actus Primus. Scœna Prima'*, introduced, presumably by the printer or those preparing the manuscripts, to make the book look more prestigious or literary, and to maintain a uniform typographical style throughout. *Antony and Cleopatra* is one of these, and the act and scene divisions introduced in modern editions do not entirely reflect the empty stage convention.

Some classically minded Elizabethan writers, including Ben Jonson, particularly in those plays he revised specifically for printed publication, make a formal scene division whenever a new character enters, even if there is no break in the action or change of location. This can help readers' recognition of which character is on stage, but hinder their understanding of the shape of the scene, and it does not reflect theatrical experience.

Scenic structure – case study: *Othello*

The story of *Othello* has what critics have famously called a 'double time scheme'. Othello and Desdemona have married secretly in Venice. That night Othello is called to the Senate in order to be sent immediately to defend the island of Cyprus from the Turks. Arrangements are made for Iago to accompany Desdemona in another ship with his wife, Emilia, as her maid. Othello's lieutenant, Cassio, travels on a third ship. Othello and Desdemona therefore spend their wedding night on Cyprus, but the following morning, Iago convinces Othello that Desdemona is having an affair with Cassio. Othello orders Cassio's murder and, that night, kills his wife. It is pretty unbelievable, and many readers have been unable to accept the sudden onset of Othello's jealousy. But Cassio – who, we're told by Iago, also has a 'fair wife' back in Florence – has been visiting a prostitute on Cyprus, Bianca. She complains that he has kept 'a week away' from her. More than simply introducing a second physical time scheme, her speech introduces a third, psychological one:

> What, keep a week away? seven days and nights?
> Eightscore eight hours? and lovers' absent hours
> More tedious than the dial eight score times?
> O weary reckoning.
>
> (*Othello*, 3.4.174–7)

Shakespeare has used the same idea in the earlier play *As You Like It*, where there is 'no clock in the forest' (3.2.284). There, the heroine, Rosalind, in disguise, instructs the young man she loves in the relativity of time:

> Time travels in divers paces with divers persons. I'll tell you who Time ambles withal, who Time trots withal, who Time gallops withal, and who he stands still withal … he trots hard

with a young maid between the contract of her marriage and
the day it is solemnised; if the interim be but a se'nnight, Time's
pace is so hard that it seems the length of seven year.

(As You Like It, 3.2.289–98)

In *Othello*, this idea becomes a plot device. It is important that
the audience should be absolutely certain that Desdemona is
innocent. We must be prevented from giving any credence to
Iago's lies, and one way of doing that, irrefutable because it is
mechanistic, is to ensure that she has had no time to commit
adultery. Conversely, an audience also has to be convinced that
Othello's jealousy, if not reasonable, is at least understandable.
This psychological duration of time works its magic in a fourth
time scheme – the real time, playing time, of the theatre –
through Shakespeare's control of scenic structure.

The play has fifteen scenes. The central scene, in which we
see Othello on his first morning on Cyprus, going about his
essential duties as commander of the island, sending letters back
to Venice, and preparing to inspect the fortifications, is just six
lines long (3.2). This little scene is a pivot, because these are the
last military acts we see him perform. The second half of the
play is devoted entirely to the piecemeal destruction of his
private life.

The first half of the play has been used to establish Othello's
quiet and absolute authority as a general; we see him on two
occasions preventing skirmishes amongst the Venetians.
Throughout that first half, he also demonstrates his ability to
hold his public life and his private life in balance. It is the tales
of his public life as a soldier that have so excited Desdemona,
while even in his speeches to the senate (particularly 1.3.260–74)
he has combined care for their demands with care for her.

The first half of the play has also been used to demonstrate
Iago's skills in manipulation. We see him extorting money out
of Roderigo (who, he says, still has a chance of marrying

Desdemona), running rings round Desdemona's father, Brabantio, and destroying Cassio's career by getting him drunk on duty. Although Iago is plotting to destroy Othello from the very beginning, it is only in the second half of the play that he has got himself into the position where he is ready to start to work on Othello himself.

Because Shakespeare was writing for a theatre with minimal staging, he was able to use the stage rather like a screen writer: the same group of characters in the same scene can apparently move in and out of public spaces, or the focus of the dialogue can shift between different groups of characters on the stage, even apparently delving deep into the 'mind' of a character through the use of soliloquy. Characters may sometimes lie to each other, but in soliloquy they always tell us exactly what they think.

These various techniques are all employed in the two scenes in which Iago sets out to destroy Othello, and are particularly apparent in 3.3, which at over 480 lines is one of the longest Shakespeare ever wrote. But it is not just its length that makes it appear long. This scene is constructed like a chain. When a group of characters leaves the stage, they always leave at least one character behind who is then shortly met on stage by others. Rather than giving us eight or nine separate scenes, there is just one, and the effect is that Iago appears never to let Othello off the hook.

Everyone on Cyprus loves and esteems Iago as an honest man and a dependable soldier. Othello has fought with him 'At Rhodes, at Cyprus, and on other grounds' (1.1.29). He is a man to be trusted. Soldiering depends on trusting your fellow soldiers; immensely strong personal bonds develop between those who fight together, perhaps stronger than any normal ties of love since lives really do depend on them. But the other characters have not spent the first half of the play watching him at work, as we have done. There is a huge discrepancy between what we know and what they know, and 'discrepant awareness', to use the term coined by the critic Bertrand Evans, both between characters and between any individual character's knowledge and what the audience knows, is an important factor in understanding how the play as a whole works. We have heard Iago tell us he is going to destroy Othello and we have seen him manipulating and destroying Roderigo and Cassio. Shakespeare's task now in this scene is to try to get us to experience Othello's changing state of mind, and this is why he strings out the scene. The atmosphere is relentless.

The scene begins in a semi-public space, where people come and go. Desdemona, urged on by Emilia, who says that Iago would support it, promises Cassio that she will get him reinstated as Othello's lieutenant. Cassio then sees Othello and Iago coming, and takes his leave. The focus shifts to Iago who pointedly draws Othello's attention to Cassio's exit. Then the two groups break and reform: Desdemona draws her husband into conversation – about Cassio. Teasingly she makes him agree that Cassio should come to dinner:

> I wonder in my soul
> What you would ask me that I should deny,
> Or stand so mammering on.

> (3.3.69–71)

She continues in this vein for another thirteen lines, not just until he agrees (which takes about thirty lines from when she first broaches the subject) but until he completely capitulates, if for no other reason (presumably) than that he really does need to get on with some work:

> I will deny thee nothing
> Whereon I do beseech thee grant me this,
> To leave me but a little to myself.

> (3.3.84–6)

She and Emilia leave the stage, but he is not allowed to work. Carefully, and bit by bit, Iago too broaches the subject of Cassio, checking how long Othello has known him, and dropping one-word comments such as 'Indeed' that make it look as if he knows something that Othello does not. Othello tells us that Iago has frowned – did 'contract and purse thy brow together' – as if he knows something that troubles him. Iago risks making Othello angry by refusing to tell him what he 'knows', insisting that he has a right to his own 'thoughts' and that he may be wrong in his suppositions, before launching into a seven-line speech about reputation – with the implication that as an 'honest' man he does not want to slander Cassio (3.3.91–168).

Although Othello has not yet uttered one jealous word, Iago tells him to beware of 'the green-ey'd monster' and tells him: 'That cuckold lives in bliss' who knows what his wife is up to, but does not love her, whereas the husband who loves but suspects, lives in torment, counting 'damned minutes'; again, we are reminded of the painful slowness of time experienced by those in extreme emotional states. The question Iago poses, however, is not *whether* the woman is unfaithful, but whether the husband *knows* about it; there is no question but that she is guilty. This dialogue between them has taken about eighty lines, a not insignificant amount of stage time, and already longer than many Shakespearean scenes, but it is not over yet. Othello announces that it is not his way to live in doubtful jealousy:

> 'Tis not to make me jealous
> To say my wife is fair, feeds well, loves company,
> Is free of speech, sings, plays, and dances well;
> Where virtue is, these are more virtuous.

(3.3.187–90)

Then comes the tiniest piece of self-doubt about his own 'weak merits', for 'She had eyes and chose me', before the assertion 'I'll see before I doubt; when I doubt, prove', and the firm decisiveness that has made him such a good general:

> And on the proof, there is no more but this –
> Away at once with love or jealousy.
>
> (3.3.195–6)

Iago appears pleased, even relieved. He can now speak his mind more frankly. He has no proof, he says, but Othello should 'observe' Desdemona with Cassio; he makes the common seventeenth-century observation about the 'pranks' of Venetian women, and with pinpoint accuracy states, 'She did deceive her father, marrying you'. He reiterates his love and duty, begs Othello's pardon for having 'dashed' his spirits, and when Othello denies that he is 'moved', insists that he must not 'strain' his speech to 'grosser' issues. His every word is an insinuation. Othello repeats his belief in his wife's honesty, 'I do not think but Desdemona's honest', but the double negative 'not ... but' construction reveals a chink of doubt. Iago hits on the word 'think'; 'Long live she so, and long live you to think so'. Othello perhaps scarcely hears him, because he is now beginning to think about 'nature erring from itself'. Iago breaks in on this, shifting the focus from Desdemona's honesty to her relationships with other men: she has erred from herself as a Venetian, he says, by marrying a black man. Othello immediately dismisses him, but asks him to 'Set on thy wife to observe'. Iago takes his leave just long enough for Othello to regret that he ever got married, before returning to urge him not to give Cassio his place back too soon: 'Note if your lady strain his entertainment ... Much will be seen in that'. There is repeated stress on the sense of sight (3.3.197–260).

Othello is now at last left alone on stage. In soliloquy he remarks on Iago's honesty. He states that if he can prove Desdemona unfaithful he will cast her off, but then he reflects on the reasons why she might not love him: he is black; cannot make polite conversation; is getting old. These self-doubts give way to the assumption that 'she is gone ... and my relief / Must be to loathe her', and the explanation that it is the curse of 'great ones' to attract such a mate (3.3.262–81). Then Desdemona, accompanied by Emilia, returns to call him to dinner. The sight of her rekindles his love. He speaks faintly and excuses this by saying he has a headache. She offers to bind his head with her handkerchief, which he resists: 'Your napkin is too little'. In her concern for him she does not notice that it has fallen to the ground.

Othello and Desdemona leave the stage, and Emilia steps forward to pick up the handkerchief. She tells us that it is a much-prized love token (3.3.294–9). We, and indeed Desdemona, will only learn later that it was given by an Egyptian sibyl to Othello's mother as a guarantee of his father's love, and that its design of strawberries is embroidered with thread said to be dyed with the mummy made from maidens' hearts: 'To lose't or give't away were such perdition/As nothing else could match' (3.4.55–68). Whether or not we believe Othello (or believe the sibyl) Shakespeare uses this little piece of woven cloth to link and contrast the different male–female relationships in the play. It passes between each of its three couples: Othello and Desdemona; Emilia and Iago; and Cassio and Bianca. In doing so, it raises the prospect of happily married love for all three of the women, while creating mayhem. Othello says 'there's magic in the web of it' (3.4.55–78). Be that as it may, it provokes the most basic and intense of human emotions, and in becoming the instrument for Iago's plot becomes the concrete manifestation of the 'net' that earlier he has promised will 'enmesh them all' (2.3.350–1). It is typical of Shakespeare's control of his material that he is able to integrate imagery, metaphor, and stage prop in this way.

All Emilia sees is a handkerchief, but since Iago wants it so much, she hopes that she can win back his love if she gives it to him – their relationship throughout is clearly unsatisfactory. She would not be so dishonest as to steal it, but if it's lying around, why not? 'I nothing but to please his fantasy' (3.3.303). Iago enters and she teases him: 'I have a thing for you' – both a promise of the 'thing' he wants, and a sexual offer, which he coldly rejects. Undaunted she produces the handkerchief. An eighteenth-century stage direction here, followed by all modern editors, instructs him to 'snatch' it, but Iago's words suggest something much more interesting: 'good wench, give it me' (3.3.317). How much more cruel it would be if he pretends just for a moment that he is interested in her, and she willingly gives it to him in a loving embrace, before he pockets it and dismisses her.

Iago now has a tangible object, a prop, which he can use in some carefully stage-managed event to give Othello the 'ocular proof' he is demanding. The remaining 140 lines of the scene are used to chip away further at Othello's sense of self and to bring him to see the handkerchief in Cassio's hand in his imagination, so that when he sees it in Cassio's hand for real in the next scene he believes what he is being told.

Our understanding of what we see is easily manipulated, as any stage magician knows, by being prevented from seeing the whole picture. Accordingly, most of the scenes in this play take place at night – the whole of Act 1; 2.2 and 2.3; and then from the end of 4.2 right through to the finish. This is unusual, because on the day-lit, Elizabethan stage, night could only be represented by characters bringing on more light – lanterns, candles, or torches. The characters in this play frequently cannot quite see, either actually or metaphorically, what is clearly before our eyes. Even in daytime scenes, vision is obscured – by the storm in 2.1 – or distorted, as when Iago tells Othello to 'encave' himself. This places him within sight but out of earshot of the dialogue between Iago and Cassio concerning the handkerchief, which would otherwise enable him to interpret what he sees correctly (4.1.79). Characters see what they expect to see – even Iago, who confidently misidentifies messengers from the Duke as Brabantio and his household, because that is what he has arranged (1.2.29).

Probable impossibility

One reason why Shakespeare's plays appear to represent reality is that they use language in a circular way. He repeats events, situations, and individual words or word-families, or words that contain similar sounds. Words such as sight/insight, natural/nature/unnatural, in *Lear* are applied to both the Lear and Gloucester families; net/web/enmesh/ensteeped/encaved/ handkerchief in *Othello* likewise give the impression of a totality of experience. They create a sense of a coherent world in which even the strangest things can seem reasonable.

Shakespeare thus seems also to have been aware of perhaps the most insightful, but also the most neglected, observation in the whole of Aristotle's *Poetics*, that in play construction a 'probable impossibility is to be preferred to an improbable possibility' (*Poetics*, xxv). In other words, realism is not the goal. It does not matter that when reduced to their storylines, most of the plays of Shakespeare seem unrealistic to the point of being daft. We get drawn into these stories because the plotting convinces us. As the play unfolds, it educates us into accepting that what we are watching is probable in that play world, no matter how unrealistic it might be in ours. Touchstone, one of Shakespeare's wisest fools whose very name implies a test for the truth, gives us the paradox: 'the truest poetry is the most feigning' (*As You Like It*, 3.3.16). Good poetry is artistically constructed (feigned) to tell us a story, which no matter how fanciful, speaks acutely to our feelings and thereby seems true.

Shakespeare often further persuades us of such truth by insisting on the theatricality of what we are watching. As Fabian says in *Twelfth Night*, 'If this were played upon a stage now, I could condemn it as an improbable fiction' (3.4.121–3). He is right; the story is ludicrous. We laugh and agree with him, and in so doing we find it all perfectly probable. But Shakespeare's primary means of achieving this feat is through his plotting: the juxtaposition of incidents, characters, and relationships, which are similar but different, and thereby provide a multi-faceted view of the given problem.

Character

Of course, what we see when we go to the theatre (and also what we see when we read and try to imagine the action) is not the plot but the characters. An Oxford don, at a touring performance of *Othello* given by Shakespeare's company, describes, in Latin, the power of the actors to move him to tears, and particularly:

> Desdemona killed by her husband, although she always acted the matter very well, in her death moved us still more greatly; when lying in bed she implored the pity of those watching with her countenance alone.

This is a very striking and empathetic reaction, although even so we do not know what if any moral meaning he attributed to this character in the play.

When it comes to Othello himself, traditional character criticism has been divided between those who see a 'noble moor' and those who see a savage wife-beater. These judgements may partly reflect potential racism in the critic (whether race hatred or a love of the exotic) but are mostly the result of the ambivalence with which the character is presented in the play. To jealous Roderigo, he is the 'extravagant and wheeling stranger/Of here and everywhere' (1.1.137–8). But to Iago, who is trying to convince Roderigo of his own capability, Othello will 'as tenderly be led by the nose/As asses are' (1.3.395–6). Othello, however, regards himself as absolutely constant and decisive like the Propontic sea, which flows inexorably and without ebb into the Hellespont (3.3.457–60). All are true, but none completely so.

Character study in literary criticism went out of the window in the 1970s and 80s. This was partly because of a growing interest in the social and political context for literature, and partly because a better understanding of human psychology had shown us that individual character is not fixed. It is not simply that people change or 'develop' with age and experience, or that certain adult behaviours can be ameliorated by unpicking or 'analysing' childhood trauma; rather, that we all behave differently in different contexts. Where, then, does character lie?

Like other writers of his period, Shakespeare sometimes borrows stock characters from the *commedia dell'arte* tradition – the old man, the braggart soldier – but in order to create the illusion of reality, he uses the same techniques of complexity, duplication, and repetition-with-difference that he employs in his plots. He will place more than one character in the same or similar position and let them take different approaches to the dilemma in which they find themselves. We hear them express their different opinions on the same theme and that encourages us to question what the best approach to that problem might be. It is this that keeps us interested in these plays when the works from which he culled so much material are more or less forgotten.

Characterisation is therefore a kind of illusion created by the play's structure and its genre. A character in a play consists only in what we hear and see them say and do, combined with our judgement – shaped by the play's structure – of what other characters say about them. For example, what Iago says about

Othello in soliloquy is probably true; what he tells the other characters in dialogue depends on the demands of his own plot. A character is therefore a construction of the writing and has no other existence. It is worth stressing this point because students commonly declare that a phrase 'reveals' some aspect of character — as if the character exists in some fuller sense in a limbo separate from the text, and that the skill of the dramatist lies in his ability to draw down this fully formed personage to incorporate it in his play.

Repetition-with-difference – case study: the character of Hamlet

The phrase 'like *Hamlet* without the prince' is a common response to a situation where something is felt to be missing. I want to turn that on its head: our understanding of the character of Hamlet cannot exist without the play. Shakespeare's play gives us five young people who have to face up to the traumatic loss of a father: Hamlet himself, whose father, King Hamlet, has been murdered by his uncle Claudius; Ophelia, Hamlet's beloved, and Laertes, her brother, whose father, Polonius, is accidentally murdered by Hamlet; Fortinbras, whose father, the King of Norway, was killed in combat with Hamlet's father; and, in the speech performed by a group of travelling players when they first arrive at Elsinore, Pyrrhus, whose father Achilles was slain by Paris during the siege of Troy.

Each of these characters responds differently. Ophelia goes mad and kills herself. Fortinbras prepares for war. Pyrrhus is one of the Greeks inside the Trojan horse and runs through the town killing all he meets until he finds King Priam. Laertes, enraged by his father's death, returns at the head of a mob, demanding Claudius's blood. Ironically, though Claudius is the true cause of the problems in Denmark, Laertes has identified him for no particular reason, and is easily deflected into wanting to kill Hamlet instead, declaring he would 'cut his throat i'th'church'. Perhaps even Claudius is momentarily shocked by this readiness to defile a place of worship before agreeing that 'No place indeed should murder sanctuarise./Revenge should have no bounds' (4.7.126–8). Instead, he flatters him into agreeing to fight Hamlet in a duel, in which he will be provided with an 'unbated' (unblunted) sword. Perhaps less confident of his boasted ability when push comes to shove, Laertes states that he will also bait or dip the point of this sword in poison he has already bought from a mountebank.

Hamlet toys with many, but not all, of these courses of action. He plays at being mad, and believes he must take revenge, coming close to it when he comes across Claudius not in church but at prayer. But he stops himself in mid strike to ponder his action, and stands for fourteen lines motionless with his sword drawn. This gives us time to recall the player's speech (and no doubt his similar motionless gesture) as he describes Pyrrhus in the moment before Priam's murder:

> his sword,
> Which was declining on the milky head
> Of reverend Priam, seemed i'th'air to stick.
> So, as a painted tyrant, Pyrrhus stood,
> And, like a neutral to his will and matter,
> Did nothing.
>
> (2.2.471–6)

Pyrrhus is a '*painted* tyrant' both because he is motionless, like a figure in a painting, and because he is covered in Trojan blood. But he is a tyrant either way in killing a defenceless old man. The play thus gives us three parallel images and tacitly asks us whether we really want our Hamlet to be like either the bloody and cold-blooded Pyrrhus or the unthinking, hotheaded, but also curiously devious Laertes.

The reason of course that Hamlet gives for not killing Claudius at that moment is not that it is wrong to kill someone at prayer, but that his revenge would not be perfect: Claudius, praying, would go to heaven. Then Hamlet leaves the stage and Claudius rises, admitting that his thoughts are preventing him from praying properly: 'words without thoughts never to heaven go' (3.3.103). Hamlet's reason for not killing him is thus invalidated. Emotionally, we might regret that he has missed his opportunity – and many critics have blamed him for not acting. But while it adds to the sense of chance in the play, this new information still does not invalidate the structural comparisons that the *plot* makes with Pyrrhus and Laertes.

Our sense of the rounded complexity of the character of Hamlet is created by the juxtaposition of so many single-faceted examples of characters in a similar predicament. But more than that, the play shows that each of these characters' individual reactions is inadequate, or morally wrong, or both. It thereby gets us involved in wondering what an acceptable and effective solution might look like. It encourages us to think thoughts that are nowhere expressed in the play – except elliptically by faithful, thoughtful Horatio who, to Hamlet's annoyance, casts doubt on the rightness of sending Rosencrantz and Guildenstern to their deaths. 'So Rosencrantz and Guildenstern go to't' is Horatio's quiet comment, which prompts an angry outburst from Hamlet, 'Why man, they did make love to this employment; They are not near my conscience' (5.2.56–8). Horatio does not reply except to shift the dialogue to the subject of Claudius. We might excuse Hamlet's act as a form of self-defence amounting at most to manslaughter – like his killing of Polonius. Horatio's silence reminds us that in such a world, such acts might be inevitable, but they are still not things to be dismissed lightly.

Revenge killing is never a solution. It invariably sets in motion a train of ever more deaths. After all, by killing

Polonius, Hamlet has become in turn the object of a son's revenge. The play which began with an armed figure, the ghost of King Hamlet, stalking the battlements, ends with an armed figure, the warlike Fortinbras, bidding the soldiers shoot as Hamlet's body is carried 'to the stage'. This seems to promise strong and stable government, but it marks a return to a previous age, and a likely continuation of an endless, pointless cycle of competing claims. Fortinbras has 'rights of memory' in Denmark, lost when his father was defeated by King Hamlet, but which his present 'vantage' allows him to claim – for now, perhaps, until some counter-claimant comes along (5.2.381–2). The play is a tragedy not just because Hamlet is dead, but because of that depressing return to normality, and the loss of the potential for change that Hamlet had briefly represented.

Starring roles and bit parts

In *Hamlet* it is not difficult to see that the other characters contribute to our understanding of Hamlet himself. But the earlier play *Richard III* is focused more relentlessly on Richard himself and is usually regarded as simply a star vehicle. Sometimes this gets translated into production choices. In a famous RSC production, Antony Sher's extraordinary ability to bound across the stage on crutches was reinforced by a costume with long, almost floor-length pointed sleeves so that at rest, leaning on those crutches, he looked like a malevolent insect on six legs. The rest of the cast, however, were costumed all in grey, making it difficult to distinguish between them.

If we have learnt anything from the Globe Theatre reconstruction in London, however, it is that audience comprehension depends on being able to see characters actively listening to what is being said, even if they cannot always see the character

speaking. Richard's long tirade in 1.3 depends on being punctu-
ated by the bemused reactions of the characters around him,
which he cuts off mid sentence. His energy feeds off theirs,
because of course, politically, he is also dependent on them
doing what he wants them to do. 'What say the citizens?' asks
Richard when Buckingham comes from the meeting at the
Guildhall where the burghers of London are supposed to agree
to him becoming king. Buckingham replies in some exaspera-
tion: 'Now by the holy Mother of our Lord, / The citizens are
mum, say not a word.' (3.7.1–3). Being 'mum' is an expression
of fear, and also a kind of stubborn resistance. In his previous
scene, Buckingham had been cockily confident that his oratory
would sway them; his failure now is dangerous for him. It is now
he who is verbose, enumerating all the arguments he has just
made to the citizens, and Richard who listens. It is the beginning of the end for Buckingham.

Thus, the most important feature of *Richard III* is not so
much Richard's relentless plots, or Margaret's death knell
rhetoric, 'I had an Edward, till a Richard killed him … Thou
hadst a Richard, till a Richard killed him' (4.4.39–42), but the
silence of the people. And for me, the single most important
character is the unnamed scrivener who has a fourteen-line
scene all to himself, a sonnet on the abuse of power (albeit
constructed in four groups of three blank verse lines plus a
couplet, rather than three groups of four rhymed lines plus a
couplet). It is he who has been given the seemingly unimportant
job of copying out the indictment of Lord Hastings so that it can
be displayed in public. It has taken him a long time, longer, in
fact, than the time taken to arrest and execute Hastings himself.

> Who is so gross
> That cannot see this palpable device?
> Yet who so bold but says he sees it not?
> (3.6.10–12)

It is in just such everyday, low-level acts by ordinary people, who can see what is happening but do nothing to stop it, that tyranny is enabled to flourish.

Shakespeare and women

One of the more contentious aspects of Shakespeare's character-isation has been his treatment of his women characters. Critics tell us that Elizabethan society expected women to be silent. Clearly that is what Desdemona's father expects too – a 'maiden never bold' (*Othello*, 1.3.94). What we see and hear in that play, however, is a woman prepared, and able, to speak eloquently to the senate, demanding to accompany her husband into a war zone.

It is of course possible to point to any number of tracts written in the period demanding women's silent obedience, although, of course, the writers of these tracts might not have felt compelled to pen them with such frequency had women in real life not been quite noisy. Occasionally, and much to our relief, a woman writes a robust rejoinder, but the spoken inter-actions in private family settings are of course lost to us. We do not really know how ordinary women behaved, but Shakespeare's most attractive heroines are those who speak volubly and with wit.

In highly regulated societies, exuberance easily becomes law-breaking, and the sixteenth-century church 'bawdy court' records are full of accusations of, and depositions by, those who do not conform. Even through the lens of official record-keeping, citizens' verbatim statements about what they have said and heard, including those by women, are vivid and memorable. Similarly, one of the carved misericord seats in the choir in Stratford-upon-Avon parish church shows a woman grabbing some man by the beard and beating him about the head with a saucepan. On one level this is a conventional moral warning about shrewish scolds. On another, it lets the genie out of the bottle; women can be actors, even violent actors, in their own stories.

The exact manifestation of women's behaviour today may be different – and different too in different countries in the world – but the problem has not gone away. On the day of writing this sentence, the *Guardian* newspaper reports the airbrushing of the only two women ministers out of photographs of the Israeli cabinet; the whipping of a seventeen-year-old girl for illegal sexual activity in Pakistan; and *three* stories, including a two-page spread, in the main section of the paper, on the dress sense of the eighteen wives of the G20 leaders at a summit in London (4 April 2009). None of the three bemused reporters can quite believe that she has taken on (or been given) that last assignment.

Because plays are about conflict, and are usually unmediated by a narrator telling you what to think, they afford scope for difference of opinion, both between characters, and within the same character at different moments in the play. Lear might exclaim about Cordelia 'her voice was ever soft, / Gentle and low – an excellent thing in woman' (*King Lear*, 5.3.271–2) but the irony of his position, and the cause of the tragedy, is that he was previously angry with her for *not* speaking.

In the comedies, notoriously, Shakespeare's female characters have a tendency to put on male clothing – partly because he was writing for male actors. He makes deliberate play with this in *Cymbeline*, where the heroine/boy actor urges her servant to stop beating about the bush with his moral qualms and give her the clothes that will make the transformation:

> Nay be brief,
> I see into thy end, and am almost
> A man already.
>
> (3.4.166–8)

But more importantly freedom from skirts offers a freedom for characterisation and for female speech and behaviour, which the individual woman has often claimed, but which has most often been officially denied by society to women *en masse*. Throughout Shakespeare's work, the women characters go far beyond the confines imposed by his society. It is the reassertion of social norms over the desires of the protagonists to do something different, which is the point of his tragedies.

Case study: Desdemona

Desdemona's readiness to speak so boldly to the senate in Venice shocked eighteenth-century critics as inappropriate and indecorous to the point of unbelievability. We no longer think so, but her interchange with Iago in Cyprus as they wait for news of Othello's ship has apparently been so embarrassing that it has been passed over in near silence by criticism, and is still almost invariably cut from performance (2.1.100–65). Here is someone who is not shocked by Iago's attempts to discomfort her with his bawdy jokes against women. She has come into a military environment as the general's wife, and in his absence takes it upon herself to engage with the troops. She gives as good as she gets – better in fact, since she never reposts in kind, merely daring him to do his worst and then playfully urging her maid: 'Do not learn from him, Emilia, though he be thy husband' (2.1.161–2). She has self-confidence and wit, and willingly intervenes in matters that some would say are none of her business.

In Desdemona, Shakespeare has created an impression of a person with specific skills and attributes: she is highly talented, she 'sings, plays, and dances well' (3.3.189); she is confident and articulate; she has a strongly developed sense of duty but also a strong sense of her own will – while still unmarried and the mistress of her father's house, she goes off to attend to household affairs but returns as quickly as she can to hear Othello's tales (1.3.145–50). Her abilities, like all abilities, are morally indeterminate and have the potential to be adapted for use in a variety of circumstances, to a range of ends, moral or immoral. Desdemona herself knows this. And at the close of the scene in which she has sung a song expressing her sense of lost love, and after her maid Emilia has talked about what women might need to do sexually either to support or control their men, she has a final couplet, also commonly cut in production and passed over in criticism:

> EMILIA: And have we not affections,
>   Desires for sport, and frailty, as men have?
>   Then let them use us well; else let them know,
>   The ills we do, their ills instruct us so.
> DESDEMONA: Good night, good night. God me such uses send,
>   Not to pick bad from bad, but by bad mend.
>
>   (4.3.98–103)

Desdemona's double 'good night' is quite a firm dismissal, and an apparent rejection of Emilia's advice. Emilia should probably exit at that point, leaving Desdemona alone. But Desdemona then reflects to herself that Emilia's suggested actions might be necessary; she would 'by bad' do whatever it takes, if it would only make things better. The problem with traditional character study is that it assigns generic and moral values to characterisation, which then over-ride the character's abilities and potential. If you remove, prune, or ignore the bawdy scene with Iago, you deny the actor an important resource and make lines such as those just quoted about mending 'by bad' impossible to say.

Desdemona is caught up in a situation that is beyond her comprehension because, along with everyone else except perhaps Emilia, she trusts Iago implicitly, and because Emilia, despite that distrust, needs to please her husband. Once Iago's words have planted in Othello's imagination a picture of her having sex with Cassio, her words have no impact. Her playful volubility is reduced to 'but while I say one prayer' (5.2.88). She is not quite silenced, though, even at the moment of death; her immense capacity for empathy with other human beings over-rides all other consideration and causes her to shoulder the blame for her own death: 'Nobody, I myself' (5.2.127).

I used to think that Desdemona's strength was intended to lie in her constancy; she remains true to herself and to her sense of love for Othello even when all about her goes 'out of tune' (cf. 5.2.118). Lack of constancy in women was regularly deplored in the love lyrics of the period, and graphically expressed by Nashe in the Epistle to *The Anatomie of Absurditie* (1589): 'constancy will sooner inhabit the body of a chameleon, a tiger, or a wolf, than the heart of a woman'. On these terms, she is the ideal woman. I now think that Shakespeare himself is presenting this very constancy as part of the problem if it is not matched by equal constancy in return, and that her loving, generous line 'Be as your fancies teach you;/Whate'er you be, I am obedient' (3.3.189–90) is the nub of the tragedy.

The power of poetry is the connection it can make in sound. The word 'obedient' contains an echo of the word 'be' and thereby connects the idea of obedience with the idea of being. The nature of 'being' is of course central to the dramatist's task of creating the illusion of reality in his characters, as it is central to human fascination with *how* to be. When Hamlet, for example, says 'To be or not to be' he is not just talking about the possibility of individual suicide, but raising the whole diffi-cult 'question' of the nature and purpose (if any) of human existence, the relation between life on earth and the afterlife (if any), and in particular, how to 'be' in a corrupt and tyrannous society, since taking any kind of action against it will almost inevitably result in death – as indeed it does in the play (*Hamlet*, 3.1.56–88).

In *Othello*, the idea of being is wrapped up in the idea of marriage whereby, conventionally, two become one. The stated ideal in seventeenth-century England was the so-called 'companionate' marriage, in which both parties, albeit taking gendered roles, contributed equally to a partnership. Both Othello and Desdemona try to do this in the first part of the play, even to the extent of merging or exchanging roles: Othello's speech to the senate combines consideration for her and for state affairs in equal measure; later he will describe her as 'My fair warrior' (2.1.180). But that ideal can still make others uncomfortable. While Cassio eulogises Desdemona as 'Our great captain's captain' (2.1.74), Iago, in a seemingly identical but actually diametrically opposed comment, sees a harridan, henpecking her husband: 'Our general's wife is now the general' (2.3.305). But both observations are conventional easy assumptions about a woman's place, and equally inadequate to describe the intelligent and determined young woman we have seen.

By creating characters who are each striving to find different ways to 'be', Shakespeare brings about the conflict that convincingly drives the plot forward. The side effect to this is that the plays enable us vicariously to experience multiple ways of being and as a result to imagine our own responses. This is perhaps why so many people see themselves in Hamlet and why so much Shakespeare criticism reflects the critic, and the critic's time of writing, as much as the play.

4

Reading, hearing, and seeing Shakespeare

> He reads much,
> He is a great observer, and he looks
> Quite through the deeds of men. He loves no plays,
> As thou doest Antony; he hears no music.
>
> *(Julius Caesar, 1.2.201–4)*

Shakespeare is difficult to read, and it is often assumed that this is because the language is four hundred years old. While it is true that some words have become obsolete since he used them, and that others have subtly changed their meaning, his vocabulary as a whole is not in fact particularly unfamiliar. Indeed, since he was responsible for coining a number of individual words and phrases that are now in regular usage in English, some of his language would have appeared more unusual to his contemporaries than it does to us. Indeed, as we have seen, his new-fangledness seems to have been a factor in the satirical attacks on his early work. It would be much more accurate to say that Shakespeare's language was *always* difficult to read, and particularly to read silently, because it is, mostly, poetry.

The power of poetry is that it can compress so much into so little. This is because it is structured in lines as well as sentences – the line is a form of punctuation often used to connect and contrast ideas – while the words are chosen for their sounds and rhythms as well as their literal meanings. The joy of poetry, even when it is concerned with sad and serious subjects, is its playfulness and its capacity to mean several things at once. Trying to keep up a running translation in one's head into simple prose is therefore not possible, let alone desirable.

Shakespeare's plays are also difficult to read because they were written for performance – that is, with a view to *actors'* reading and then speaking, not for the reading enjoyment of the layman. One needs to be able to visualise the spatial arrangements between characters on the stage, and to realise that the dialogue is full of directions for action (kneeling, for example, or laying hold of someone), without these being spelled out in overt stage directions.

Many aspects of the early modern playtexts that have come down to us in print can only properly be understood if we think more about early modern theatrical practices. Prologues and epilogues were probably written for specific performances only; some may not have been written by the author or authors of the rest of the play. Most importantly, the actor's part only gave the speeches and cues for an individual character. How might this have affected the way in which the actor read, and an experienced actor-writer – like Shakespeare – wrote?

RHETORIC

The ability to communicate with and influence others is of course an essential skill for politicians and those involved in public service. Elizabethan schoolboys and students would have been taught this skill by studying the speeches and arguments of the Roman statesman and orator Cicero, and the principles of rhetoric set out by the Spanish Roman author Quintilian. Nevertheless, ever since classical times, there has also been a recognition that rhetoric can be 'flowery', even deliberately misleading, mere sophistry rather than wisdom; scorn of the lying politician is nothing new. But rhetoric is much more than a seemingly endless and daunting list of rhetorical terms and figures. Since its purpose is to influence others, it follows

RHETORIC (cont.)

that it fosters an interest in psychology. The first book on psychology written in English is Thomas Wright's *The Passions of the Mind in General* (1604), intended primarily as a work about rhetoric and speaking well. And like Quintilian, Wright also stresses the need for appropriate gesture in order to get the message across.

Speech and gesture

We tend to think about words in literature as the expression of ideas, and the description of physical things. But that is not the primary function of speech. Speech is very much more than audible words. Speech is our way of influencing others, *doing something to them*. Speech is an act.

Speech is also embodied. Spoken words are breath, and breath is both sound and bodily movement. It is not simply that gesture is a prehistoric form of communication, which was later replaced by speech, as used to be thought, but rather that sound and gesture are two sides of a single mental process. We move when we speak. Gesture develops alongside speech in the young child, and continues to provide us with possibly as much as twenty per cent additional information to that contained in words alone.

While we all naturally employ sophisticated modulation of the voice, different facial expressions and body postures, and a wealth of small gestures of the hands and arms when we speak our own words, it takes an experienced speaker to choose effective intonation and gesture when speaking someone else's words. Even then, the evidence of theatre practice down the ages, as well as the scene in which Hamlet gives advice to a company of players visiting Elsinore (*Hamlet*, 3.2), suggests that most performers need and expect rehearsal advice. It is immensely difficult to understand the richness of Shakespeare's potential for meaning without rehearsing it with other people. When we read Shakespeare silently, confined to our armchairs, we disable two aspects of ourselves, which would otherwise help with comprehension: our voice, and our body.

Gesture and stage direction

It is a truism to say that there are very few stage directions in Shakespeare's plays. But like many truisms, it is misleading. To be sure, there are few if any of the kind of overt directions that we commonly find in modern plays, for example, directing an actor to say a line 'dejectedly', or 'softly', or to 'sit at the table'. That kind of direction, along with detailed descriptions of the set, was developed for the printed editions of late nineteenth-century plays by George Bernard Shaw and Henrik Ibsen, prepared specifically with readers in mind, since theatre productions of their then very controversial works were limited. Reading a playtext without such descriptive aids to help the imagination is a particularly difficult task, not unlike reading a music score and hearing it in one's head.

The sixteenth- and seventeenth-century playtexts that have come down to us rarely contain such overt information. The snippets of theatrical business they contain tend to be more reminders for the stage keeper to prepare a prop, or for an actor to come on stage prepared in some way – either mentally, or carrying a prop – rather than descriptions of what happens once the actors are on stage. For example, in *Richard III*, the stage direction '*Enter Richard and Buckingham at several doors*' (3.7) utilises a common staging convention. It indicates that these two characters have just come from different places and are meeting with news to tell each other. Elsewhere in that play we have: '*Enter the Queen with her hair about her ears, Rivers and Dorset after her*' (2.2.33); '*Enter Lovell and Ratcliffe with Hastings' head*' (3.5.11);

'*Enter Richard aloft between two Bishops*' (3.7.94); and, my favourite, '*Enter Richard and Buckingham in rotten armour, marvellous ill-favoured*' (3.5.0). What these all have in common is that they set up meaningful visual images that are immediately borne out by the text. Lovell announces 'Here is the head of that ignoble traitor'; the Mayor observes 'See where his Grace stands between two clergymen'; and Richard and Buckingham, who should look as if they have raided the dressing-up box (or rather the motley collection of old rusty armour often kept in church store rooms for the purposes of national defence) start joking about how they are playacting being frightened, reluctant soldiers.

The Queen's dishevelled or 'torn' hair, however, is a naturalistic rather than natural mark of distress, although one that we can readily understand now. The full direction also denotes the Queen's refusal to be restrained by her two sons, who enter chasing after her. This not only ensures a certain desperate level of energy in the entrance, but gives a clear instruction to the young actor playing the Queen that he must take the initiative and set the pace. But unkempt hair also has more specific cultural meanings. It may have become a stage convention in England through familiarity with Roman literature, where it is found as a particularly female way of expressing grief. Anthony Corbeill relates it to other ritualistic gestures of child-bearing and nurturing since it was the woman's role to help the deceased into the afterlife. On the Elizabethan stage, however, it acquires a different meaning: a lack of feminine composure, a regression to childhood, even madness. We saw this in the Q1 text of *Hamlet*, when Ophelia enters to her mad scene (p. 34), while in the Folio text of *Troilus and Cressida*, Priam's daughter Cassandra enters to deliver her wild prophecy about the fall of Troy '*with her hair about her ears*' (2.2.100).

Once the actors are on stage and equipped with the props for the scene, however, they can usually rely on their lines to tell them what to do without further overt direction. This is why it is always so instructive to stand up and act out a scene. Lines that seem puzzling when read silently suddenly become clear when you start to think about where and how you as an actor are standing relative to others acting with you, and where and how you might need to move, both in response to what is said to you, and to reinforce what you are saying.

Image and movement

A good actor will feel impelled to move, both when he speaks and when he listens. He will be motivated by the images conjured up by the words and their meanings, and by their sounds and rhythms. Shakespeare's dialogue is full of striking images often involving action:

> And pity, like a naked new-born babe,
> Striding the blast, or heaven's cherubin horsed
> Upon the sightless couriers of the air,
> Shall blow the horrid deed in every eye,
> That tears shall drown the wind.
>
> (*Macbeth*, 1.7.21–5)

This is not just poetic extravagance. It offers practical theatrical help. Visualising the actions of the babe and the cherubin will help an actor give his delivery emotional power and variability. But an actor trained in classical memory techniques and carrying a mental image of a significant building or 'memory theatre' in his head, might well place images of the babe and the cherubin on different architectural features of that building. Mentally walking through it, even while performing in an unfamiliar space, would help him recall the images and therefore the speech, while also encouraging him to direct his delivery to different parts of the auditorium in front of him. He would thereby draw in the whole audience, perhaps eyeballing individuals on 'every eye'.

An Elizabethan actor would also make use of a repertoire of gestures developed in the art of oratory to convey meaning to large gatherings of people. But if he is really immersed both in what he is saying, and in what he is listening to, he is also likely to make the kinds of small gestures with the hands and arms, as well as with the face, that we all make when we speak, even without being fully aware that we are doing so.

It is likely that prehistoric man's grunts and gestures (and a pre-talking toddler's yells, body movements, and facial expressions) do not equate simply with nouns or things, but with whole sentences: not simply 'bear', but 'there is a bear behind that bush and it's coming to get me'. In that kind of stressful situation, we can all find ourselves reduced to pre-talking sound and gesture. Shakespeare writes just such a scenario into the middle of *The Winter's Tale*, couched in the most famous stage direction of all time: '*Exit pursued by a bear*'. The yells of fear that the actor playing Antigonus might want to make as he leaves the stage have been anticipated by sound effects, described in his words as an approaching storm and as 'savage clamour'. Later we will hear that the storm has wrecked the ship that has brought him to the shore, causing the 'piteous cry of the poor souls' who perished on her. The 'savage clamour' will therefore need to suggest hunt, angry bear, and shipwreck and will consist of as much noise as can be made by fourteen or so actors, their stage hands, and a motley collection of instruments, including horns, a wind machine, and the long, ridged trough and cannonball used for making thunder. These effects in broad daylight in the theatre are unlikely to be very terrifying to us – and staging the bear is often regarded as one of the more problematic features of the play. But the wild disruption that is described is then imitated in the language of the Clown, a young shepherd who enters to tell us what has happened. He has seen an extraordinarily violent storm and two terrible events, the shipwreck and the bear eating the 'gentleman'. Unable to concentrate on either event for long, he switches from one to the other. His language positively encourages acting out, with gestures to imitate and conjure up the action of the ship 'boring the moon with her mainmast, and anon swallowed with yeast and froth, as you'd thrust a cork into a hogshead' (3.3.85–100). The effect is inevitably funny. Our laughter, appropriate to the performance before us, is inappropriate to the things being described. Such contrasts of emotion, words, and actions immerse us in the contrasts of the play; as will later be said of Paulina, Antigonus's wife, 'She had one eye declined for the loss of her husband, another elevated that the oracle was fulfilled' (5.2.70). We will imagine the shipwreck and the bear's dinner with more reality than the Clown can tell them, or than they could be staged, while at the same time remaining in our present reality, hugely enjoying his over-the-top performance of imbecility.

Mood and grammar

Shakespeare's language in plays and poems alike is exciting because its changes of rhythm, pace, and momentum reinforce, and even create, changes of mood and meaning. Sometimes he juxtaposes contrasting words to create emotional clashes in the same line. Sometimes he creates a sensation of constancy by maintaining the direction and pace of line after line. He achieves these effects not only in the overall semantic sense of what he is saying, but also in the particular choices of words and phrase construction he uses to express that sense. To understand how this works we not only have to pay attention to the obvious effects of imagery, but to the small words, often overlooked, that are the nuts and bolts of any sentence. In other words, we need to look at that scary thing, grammar.

Shakespeare was living at a time of great change in grammar and sentence structure. Old grammatical forms and newer ones co-existed. There were two different ways of forming both negatives and questions, and numerous ways of representing possession. The forms thou/thy were used inconsistently as the singular for you/your, and sometimes 'thou' was also used when addressing a younger or socially inferior person. The general absence of dictionaries (apart from some pioneering attempts to aid foreign language acquisition) meant there was little practical need to regularise spelling, and no means to do so, had it been thought desirable. In the words of Jonathan Hope:

> Variation and choice seemingly everywhere, where we have virtually none. No dictionaries as we understand them, and no descriptive grammars – no false sense that writing *is* language, and speaking a casual, secondary, pale imitation. Shakespeare grew up in, wrote in, a society, which was primarily oral and aural, not one which was literate.
>
> (2003, p. 6)

All this gave Shakespeare wonderful opportunities for varying the ways in which he put words together into lines and sentences in order to create specific effects.

TAKING A LINE FOR A WALK

The artist Paul Klee famously described drawing as taking a line for a walk, and applying this idea to Shakespeare's verse can be both fun and instructive. Try reading the following two sonnets out loud while walking forwards at a steady pace, changing direction only if and when the grammar, and/or the sense, change direction. Turn on words like 'but', 'or', and temporal changes like 'now', 'then', 'anon'; keep on the same course on phrases beginning with words like 'still', 'and', 'therefore', perhaps describing a curve on 'by and by', or a slight wobble on 'varying'. If you can't quite bring yourself to do this, walk your fingers across a table, or take a pencil and paper – although it is still important to read aloud. You should find

TAKING A LINE FOR A WALK (*cont.*)

that your feet, fingers, or pencil trace a completely different pattern in each poem.

105

Let not my love be called idolatry,
Nor my belovèd as an idol show,
Since all alike my songs and praises be
To one, of one, still such and ever so.
Kind is my love today, tomorrow kind,
Still constant in a wondrous excellence;
Therefore my verse, to constancy confined,
One thing expressing, leaves out difference.
Fair, kind and true, is all my argument,
Fair kind and true, varying to other words;
And in this change is my invention spent,
Three themes in one, which wondrous scope affords.
    Fair kind and true have often lived alone
    Which three, till now, never kept seat in one.

75

So are you to my thoughts as food to life,
Or as sweet-seasoned showers are to the ground;
And for the peace of you I hold such strife
As 'twixt a miser and his wealth is found;
Now proud as an enjoyer, and anon
Doubting the filching age will steal his treasure;
Now counting best to be with you alone,
Then bettered that the world may see my pleasure;
Sometime all full with feasting on your sight,
And by and by clean starvèd for a look;
Possessing or pursuing no delight
Save what is had or must from you be took.
    Thus do I pine and surfeit day by day,
    Or gluttoning on all, or all away.

Shakespeare's poems

Shakespeare's poetry is immensely erotic and covers the full range of the human experience of, and responses to, both love and sex. But the desire to read it as code for a hidden autobiography has led to a reluctance to engage with the wordplay in the sonnets and a neglect of his narrative poems.

The two long narrative poems are both based on well-known stories in Ovid: *Venus and Adonis* comes from *Metamorphoses* (Bk. 10) and *The Rape of Lucrece* from *Fasti* (Bk. 2), although Shakespeare had clearly also read retellings of the Lucrece story in Chaucer's *The Legend of Good Women*, and John Gower's *Confessio Amantis*. But Shakespeare's versions are very much longer than any of his sources. He brings a theatrical imagination to the stories, allowing the characters to express their conflicting emotions and desires in dialogue, and enabling readers to experience this conflict as a succession of ethical problems rather than moral certainties. Published within a year of each other, they should perhaps be considered as companion pieces in dialogue *with each other*. The first is the story of a rapacious goddess who tries to seduce a reluctant, even petulant young man, who later dies while hunting a wild boar. The second recounts the rape of a chaste married woman and her subsequent suicide. Although the basic stories and their outcomes are not dissimilar, the first poem is frequently funny, and the second, both horrific and tragic. How can this be?

Our individual answers to that question are shaped by how the story is expressed, as much or more than the content of the story.

Both poems contain a digression early on, which encapsulates both the story and its tone. Just at the moment Adonis breaks free from Venus, his stallion spies a mare and bolts after her, bursting reins, girths, and bit, eager to do what his master is coy about doing:

> The strong-necked steed, being tied unto a tree,
> Breaketh his rein, and to her straight goes he.
> (*Venus and Adonis*, 263–4)

In a similar way, but to opposite effect, the very house through which Tarquin creeps on his way to Lucrece's bedchamber strains against his intended deed:

> The locks between her chamber and his will,
> Each one by him enforced, retires his ward;
> But as they open they all rate his ill,
> Which drives the creeping thief to some regard.
> The threshold grates the door to have him heard;
>   Night-wand'ring weasels shriek to see him there;
>   They fright him, yet he still pursues his fear.
> (*The Rape of Lucrece*, 302–8)

Paradoxically, in order to get the most out of the 'adult' content of these poems, we need to reawaken the delight in the patterns and sounds of language that we all had when we first started gabbling as infants. Shakespeare's use of rhyme and verse form connects words and ideas together in ways that surprise, delight, satirise, or shock, as he pushes each situation to extremes. For example, trying to dissuade Adonis from the dangerous sport of boar hunting, Venus catches herself moralising. This is such an unusual event for her that she forgets what she is saying: 'Where did I leave?' He by contrast is impatient with the older woman and wants to be off partying with his mates, but is afraid he'll stumble in the dark. The result is a ludicrously ordinary lovers' tiff:

> 'Where did I leave?' 'No matter where;' quoth he
> 'Leave me, and then the story aptly ends.
> The night is spent.' 'Why what of that?' quoth she.
> 'I am,' quoth he 'expected of my friends;

> And now 'tis dark, and going I shall fall.'
> 'In night,' quoth she 'desire sees best of all.'
> (*Venus and Adonis*, 715–20)

Venus and Adonis is written in six-line stanzas, rhyming *ababcc*. *The Rape of Lucrece* is in seven-line stanzas rhyming *ababbcc*. Known as rhyme-royal, or rime-royal, this verse form is commonly used in medieval and early modern narrative poems, but Shakespeare exploits its potential in quite unusual ways. As one reads, the first four lines in each stanza often seem complete in themselves, but then the fifth line adds something more, either stretching the idea in the first four lines to breaking point, or introducing a twist that will only be completed in the couplet. Sometimes this restlessness is accentuated through enjambment, where a line runs without a break into the next. Shakespeare thus regularly manages to pull the stanza in two directions simultaneously. The effect is to make the reader experience both the inexorability and the excruciating pain of the story, and dramatises the way Tarquin's sense of his own physical and political power is used as an affront to the laws of hospitality and morality. The following stanza, for example, takes the conventional image of the lover burning in ice and freezing in fire, and turns it into a dramatic conflict between desire and moral responsibility, an idea that will be explored at length in the poem in the aftermath of the rape:

> Thus, graceless, holds he disputation
> 'Tween frozen conscience and hot-burning will,
> And with good thoughts makes dispensation,
> Urging the worser sense for vantage still;
> Which in a moment doth confound and kill
>   All pure effects, and doth so far proceed
>   That what is vile shows like a virtuous deed.
> (*The Rape of Lucrece*, 246–52)

The sonnets

Similar ambivalences in both poetic structure and meaning can be found in the sonnets. Shakespearean sonnet form is usually described as consisting of three quatrains (four-line sections), each quatrain introducing a slightly different example of the main theme, followed by a rhyming couplet that sums up what has gone before. The Italian sonnet form (often termed Petrarchan, after the poet Francis Petrarch) has an octave, or eight-line section consisting of two quatrains, followed by a sestet of six lines, which develops or transcends the ideas developed in the octave. Shakespeare was clearly aware of the two forms and often structures the *sense* of the poem 4+4//3+3, while maintaining the three quatrains plus couplet rhyme scheme. The trick in reading, as with *Lucrece*, is to notice how the rhyme scheme variously reinforces and undercuts the sense.

The very structure of these sonnets thus warns against simple explanations. Rather than trying to identify actual people as the fair man and the dark lady, or pin down Shakespeare's sexuality, we need to pay heed to the Platonic ideas expressed in Sonnet 53, where the beloved is both 'substance' (in Platonic terms, a single idea, form, or perfection) and 'millions of strange shadows' (i.e. multiple real beings). The shadows then specified, which the perfection of the beloved is supposed to outstrip, are both Adonis *and* Helen of Troy, male and female. Both are paragons of beauty, although as we have seen with Adonis, neither is noted for the generosity and constancy that one might, ideally, look for in a lover. There is also, as Stephen Booth notes (1977 and 2000), a fleeting suggestion in the final line, which is ostensibly about the beloved's unique constancy ('unlike' all others), that s/he 'does not like' others. Again it is a question of grammar, as 'like' momentarily wobbles between adjective and verb: 'But you like none, none you, for constant heart.' Shakespeare's poetry thus captures the essence of what we all experience in love: its combined joy and heartache; its infinite possibilities, the millions we might meet and the one we hopelessly hanker after; our sense of its ideal and our experience of its limitations; its variability.

Soundscape

Shakespeare had an extensive vocabulary. But he did not use every word of it in every play, nor did he use it indiscriminately; like any artist, he gives himself a restricted palette, since that will lend the work a sense of place, mood, or coherence. A glance at a Shakespeare concordance, a book that lists all the words he used alphabetically, showing the occurrence of each word in every play, shows that a word might occur many times in one play and scarcely or not at all in another. This is probably one reason why puns are so ubiquitous in Shakespeare since a pun enables the same sound to resonate in different contexts.

Using the same word in multiple senses, and particularly using it early on in the play because of the significance it will acquire later, enables him to create a soundscape and world picture for each play. We can therefore refine what was said earlier: it is not simply that genre is established by where and how the play ends (see p. 86), but that from the very beginning, the choice of language is designed to shape audience expectations. Thus in the very first scene of *The Winter's Tale* two courtiers have a conversation in which they praise King Leontes' son, Mamillius. Camillo, Leontes' chief minister, hyperbolically claims, 'they that went on crutches ere he was born, desire yet their life to see him a man.' His opposite number, Archidamus, chief minister to the visiting king Polixenes, archly inquires 'Would they else be content to die?' (1.1.38–9). There is something not quite right here. In their praise of the young boy they have harped on old age and death. It turns out that the child they describe will himself be dead by the middle of Act 3.

In the next scene, Polixenes announces that he must go home:

> Nine changes of the wat'ry star hath been
> The shepherd's note since we have left our throne
> Without a burden.

(1.2.1–3)

This is certainly a poetic and difficult way of saying 'it's nine months since I have sat on my throne', but it is difficult for a whole set of reasons, both realistic and emblematic, that contribute enormously to the performance of the drama. Firstly he is being polite. He needs to leave; he has stayed too long; but he does not want to offend his hosts and so he talks elliptically. The convolutions here will help an actor get the necessary courtly insouciance. In performance, the actor's tone of voice and friendly gestures will help us understand that he is trying to get away, while expressing his gratitude. But secondly, Shakespeare needs him to be (unknowingly) fanning the flames of a terrible jealousy in Leontes' mind. Hermione is standing on stage, perhaps between them both, heavily pregnant. No reader could pick up the essential information of her pregnancy here. There is nothing in the dialogue or the original stage directions, but in the very next scene, which takes place on the following day, she and her ladies will comment on her condition, and she gives birth shortly afterwards. The stomach of the actor playing Hermione in the first scene will therefore be heavily padded out. As a result, it may also occur to the viewer that Polixenes' nine months sojourn in this court, expressed significantly as the 'changes of the wat'ry star' (i.e. the moon, which was also thought to govern female sexuality and the menstrual cycle), means that there has theoretically been time and opportunity for him to be the father.

If we were to attempt a psychological explanation, we could say that Polixenes has been prompted to use this imagery because off stage Hermione has made some reference to wanting her pregnancy to be over, or because of the sight of her belly. We all make such connections when we speak – sometimes unconsciously, and sometimes with embarrassing consequences. The joke, if it is one, is dressed up here in *sprezzatura*, or polite but spirited courtliness, while the familiarity would not be unreasonable since he and her husband are old friends. But even so, Leontes might hear evasion and betrayal, or worse, boastfulness. There are a number of choices that actors could make, given this material.

But Shakespeare has another, purely dramaturgical purpose for Polixenes' choice of 'shepherd', 'note', and 'burden'. Though neither readers nor audience can yet know it, these words link this opening to the second half of the play, set in the countryside of Polixenes' own kingdom, where a group of shepherds will gather to celebrate a sheepshearing, buying trinkets and ballads – songs that regularly have a 'burden' (chorus) – one of which will be about a 'usurer's wife brought to bed with nine money bags at a burden' (pregnancy; 4.4.257).

It is important for these words to echo across the play. The second half will be in a different country, a different time (sixteen years later), and a different register – comedy rather than the gathering gloom and menace of tragedy in the first half. The second half will unwind and ameliorate most, though not all, of the terrors encountered in the first. But structurally, there is a danger that it will *feel* broken-backed to the audience, as it has often seemed to readers disturbed by the breaking of the Aristotelian rules of time and place. The soundscape of the word patterns in the play is an attempt to hold it together.

Music and song

Shakespeare's dramaturgy is as much about getting the audience to feel the different emotional impacts of the story as it is about presenting the story itself. One immensely powerful way of doing that in performance, and perhaps the most difficult to imagine when reading silently, is in music. The eye can scan a song lyric in a few seconds, its refrain often reduced to 'etc' in print. In performance, however, that same song will take up a significant amount of time. It will also profoundly alter the emotional balance of a scene, or even serve to change a character's state of mind. In *Othello*, Iago's roistering drinking song 'And let me the cannikin clink', followed by a few comments on the drunkenness of the English, and by his ballad of King Stephen (2.3.64–89) is all that is needed for us to believe that Cassio becomes profoundly drunk before our very eyes. In *The Tempest*, the spirit Ariel, 'invisible', draws young Prince Ferdinand on stage in music: 'Come unto these yellow sands / And then take hands' (1.2.375–6). Ferdinand has just been shipwrecked and thinks that his father has drowned. Shakespeare has to get him over that and into a state where he is credibly able to fall in love. Again, he achieves that in the music. Ferdinand tells us that for him the transformative experience has already been going on some time:

> Sitting on a bank,
> Weeping again the King my father's wreck,
> This music crept by me upon the waters,
> Allaying both their fury and my passion
> With its sweet air.
>
> (*The Tempest*, 1.2.389–93)

Ariel's next song, 'Full fathom five thy father lies', describes the body after death, transformed to coral and pearl. In the surviving setting by Robert Johnson, who regularly composed for the

King's Men, the underlying harmonies move through several quite surprising and rather beautiful changes of key. By the end of the song, Ferdinand is quite ready to be further overturned by the appearance of Miranda, 'Most sure the goddess/On whom these airs attend' (1.2.421–2). It has taken just fifty lines.

Shakespeare, as far as we know, was not himself a musician or a composer. He would have needed to draw on the services of others to write any new music, but when it is referenced in the dialogue, or is being used by the characters for a particular purpose (and is not just incidental music as might be supplied by the theatre at the end of a performance) we can safely assume that he was responsible for plotting it into his text, and knew the kind of effect he was seeking. Sometimes he draws on an old or pre-existent song, as when Falstaff sings a snatch of the ballad 'When Arthur first in court' (*2 Henry IV*, 2.4.32). Desdemona too recalls an old song sung by her mother's maid, Barbary. This survives in two different settings, one of which has an accompaniment, which seems to imitate the sound of sighing. She is, Othello says, an accomplished musician, but such is her state of mind, she muddles the order of the stanzas and then breaks off entirely, too distressed to continue.

Sometimes, as with the song in *Cymbeline*, 'Hark, hark the lark', the surviving musical setting has words that do not entirely correspond to the words in the printed text (2.3.20–7). In that case, it may have been the composer, probably again Robert Johnson, who cut the lines to fit his musical idea. He has, nevertheless, exactly captured the play's mixture of extreme styles. His setting presents in musical notes the particular soaring trill of a lark as it ascends, juxtaposed against the grandeur of the rising sungod, Phoebus. It is, as befits the mix of ancient Britain and renaissance Italy in the play, Italianate in style but also rather bombastic. The situation in the play is that Cloten the comic, but dangerous, villain has employed a professional singer. His intent is that the song will 'penetrate' the Princess Imogen and she will appear in response to the repeated summons to 'arise' – the singer, no doubt, making a grand final gesture in the direction of her bedchamber off stage. Wonderfully, of course, nothing happens; she has more sense. It falls spectacularly flat – but hilariously so for us.

It is rare, however, that one hears these particular musical examples in modern performance; theatres tend to commission new music so as to integrate the sound design with the production as a whole. They are not wrong to do so; the production needs to have coherence. But there is something to be said for analysing the likely effects of these early settings in order to translate them into modern idioms.

Verse forms, rhythm, and metre

if you mouth it, as many of our players do, I had as lief the town crier spoke my lines

(*Hamlet*, 3.2.4)

We are often taught that Shakespeare reserves poetry for his higher-class characters and makes his plebs speak prose. This is not, even in itself, entirely accurate; there are plenty of occasions in the plays when the gentles speak prose. But it deafens us to the dramaturgical power of different forms of verse and prose. We are also firmly told that Shakespeare's verse is constructed in iambic pentameter lines. Pentameter means literally 'five measures', and an iamb is a measure consisting of a short syllable followed by a long syllable (de dum or ` -), hence de dum, de dum, de dum, de dum, de dum. Again, this is a truism that is not entirely true. For although the iambic pentameter provides the beat that does indeed underlie most of his poetry, Shakespeare is careful not to make the rhythm of his words coincide exactly with this metre for too long, because more than a few lines of unrelieved iambics can have the effect of sending people to sleep.

Much mid-sixteenth-century poetry is syllabic: the alternating eight-syllable and six-syllable lines of ballad form; the fourteener; or the alternating twelve- and fourteen-syllable lines of poulter's measure. Shakespeare too uses such forms when he wishes his speakers to appear old-fashioned, such as for the ghosts of Posthumus's family in *Cymbeline* (5.4.30–92). But many writers from Chaucer onwards had tried to make English more 'fit' for poetry by trying to channel it into what they understood as Latin forms. The problem is that in Latin, sense is not determined by word order as it is in English, and words can be arranged relatively easily to fit predetermined metrical patterns of long and short syllables. Latin poetry is quantitative. But it is very difficult to pronounce a long syllable in English without giving it a stress – hence our common definition of iambic as 'unstress, stress'. Indeed, English is sometimes described as stress-timed, which means that in ordinary speech, stressed syllables seem to occur at roughly equal intervals of time, no matter how many unstressed syllables there are between them, or indeed even if there are no intervening unstressed syllables. English poetry is therefore accentual, and even where an author is aiming at a regular number of stresses or accents per line, it may have irregular numbers of syllables. Stressed and unstressed syllables may alternate in English much of the time, which is why the iamb is often said to fit, but it is not the way the language actually works.

As a grammar school boy, Shakespeare would have been familiar with William Lyly's Latin grammar. In the last section on prosody, Lyly explains that if a word that ends in a vowel is followed by a word that begins with a vowel, the first vowel is elided (i.e. suppressed or slid into the second). On the other hand, if a vowel occurs before two consonants, whether in the same word or two consecutive words, the vowel is deemed to be long, no matter its length in natural prose pronunciation. Lyly recommends that a verse speaker should always hear the metre thus artificially produced, while pronouncing the natural prose rhythms of the words. In other words, Elizabethan schoolboys were taught to hear two rhythms simultaneously: the metrical pattern, and the prose rhythm of the words.

When we first meet the pedantic schoolmaster Holofernes in *Loves Labours Lost*, he is remembering some lines of the poetry of 'Mantuan' – the poet Johannes Baptista Spagnolo. He clearly adores poetry for its sound and musicality. When a love poem written by one of the play's young aristocrats falls into his hands, he asks his friend, the village priest Sir Nathaniel, to read it. He is dismayed by what he first assumes to be the priest's wooden delivery of the poem: 'You find not the apostrophus [elision of syllables] and so miss the accent'. He snatches the poem back and prepares to show him how it should be read, but then exclaims with some disdain 'Here are only numbers ratified; but for the elegancy, facility, and golden cadence of poetry, caret' (4.2.89–115). In other words, the poem is too regular. It is impossible to release rhythm from it because the pattern created by its individual words coincides with the metre too exactly. It is in fact truly execrable verse, written in iambic hexameters – six iambs to the line, which serves to accentuate its 'de dum, de dum' quality – made yet more clunking because the content of the poem also consists of bald lists of unconnected things.

Stress patterns in Shakespeare

In ordinary English speech, syllables are stressed according to the emphasis or emotional sense that a speaker wishes to convey. As a result, vowel sounds in the unstressed syllables are compressed, thereby affecting the pronunciation of the words. Shakespeare had a good ear, and uses rhetorical patterns to influence the stress patterns that a speaker might employ, so that (unless writing deliberately bad verse) the resulting word rhythms dance above the underlying metrical beat, sometimes coinciding with it, and sometimes pulling against it.

Thus, for example, in the line 'To be or not to be that is the question' (*Hamlet*, 3.1.56) the key idea (or 'question') really 'is' that of 'being'; the important words coincide with the stress pattern of the iambic pentameter (albeit with an extra unstressed syllable at the end of the line) and 'be' is pronounced 'bee' both times. But earlier, Polonius has counselled his son, 'Be thou familiar, but by no means vulgar' (1.3.61). Here the important idea is the antithesis between familiarity and vulgarity. The metre underpins that rhetorical structure since 'familiar', 'vulgar', and the negatives 'but' and 'no' are all placed in stressed positions:

> `   _   `   _ `   _   `   _   `   _ `
>
> Be thou familiar, but by no means vulgar

But a performer would probably not want to say the line like that. Instead, he might introduce a break after 'familiar' in order to draw out the contrast with 'vulgar'; indeed, unlike most modern editions, the Folio text has a semi-colon rather than a comma at this point. In order to accommodate this, the speaker's sense of stress timing which will have already compressed the 'iar' of 'familiar' into one syllable, will turn 'Be' almost to 'bi', while removing the metrical stress from 'thou'. The result might be something like:

> `   `   `   _ `   // `   `   _   `   _ `
>
> Be thou familiar,   but by no means vulgar

Metre is therefore not the complete recipe for performance it is sometimes said to be; it is the pulse or beat that underpins but does not dictate the rhythm of the words. A performer might be well advised to give just three main stresses in this line (on the words familiar, no, and vulgar). The break in the middle, demanded by the rhetorical pattern and sense of the words, could be as long as two beats, thus enabling the line to keep time with the underlying five beats of the metre.

The only way for a dramatist to influence a speaker's accent is through the precise disposition of individual words and rhetorical patterns within the line and the sentence. A dramatist with Shakespeare's technical facility and experience as an actor, might be expected to try to write the accent of emotion into his poetry in order to create a sense of characterisation. Shakespeare's frequent departure from a strict tally of regularly alternating stressed and unstressed syllables for each line therefore needs to be considered as part of that dramaturgical technique.

An interesting example occurs in Malvolio's line at the end of *Twelfth Night*, where the important idea is revenge. It comes in response to a prose speech from Feste and is usually presented as prose in modern editions. It is certainly not regular verse, although it is highly rhythmic and it is followed by the other characters' return to emollient, regular iambic pentameter:

[FESTE:] And thus the whirligig o' time brings in his revenges.
MALVOLIO: I'll be revenged on the whole pack of you.
OLIVIA: He hath been most notoriously abused.
DUKE: Pursue him and entreat him to a peace.

(5.1.363–6)

The rhetorical structure here is the antithesis between time's revenges in general in Feste's line, and Malvolio's revenge more specifically on all the other characters. The important words and phrases for him are therefore: I'll; revenged; whole; pack of you.

A native English speaker would probably stress 'pack' and compress the vowel sound in 'you' to something approaching 'yu', which, in combination with the explosive 'p' and 'ck' sounds in pack would also express disgust. The idea of revenge is doubly shocking, coming as it does at the 'happy' end of this comedy, and might warrant a pause after it to let the shock sink in. The result could be something like:

I'll be reveng'd   on the whole pack of you.

Again, the four stresses and the pause mean that the line can be delivered exactly within the beats of an iambic pentameter line, the third beat coinciding with the pause. It thus dovetails perfectly between Feste's prose and the regular iambic verse that follows, while marking Malvolio's dissent not just in what he says, but the very way he says it.

Approached in this way both as characterisation and as aural information for audiences, Leontes' outbursts of overwhelming jealousy in the opening scene of *The Winter's Tale* are not as incomprehensible as they have appeared to generations of readers and editors. Here is a man who is collapsing into mental turmoil. We should not expect him to be speaking in complete sentences or regular verse, and the emendations that editors have often made to the text are quite unnecessary. The following modernises the spelling and capitalisation, but otherwise preserves the Folio words and punctuation:

Most dear'st, my collop: can thy dam, may't be
Affection? thy intention stabs the centre.
Thou do'st make possible things not so held,
Communicat'st with dreams (how can this be?)
With what's unreal: thou coactive art,
And fellow's nothing. Then 'tis very credent,
Thou mayst co-join with something, and thou do'st

(And that beyond commission) and I find it
(And that to the infection of my brains,
And hardening of my brows.)

$$(1.2.137-46)$$

Leontes has just been engaged in fatherly care for his son –
wiping the child's nose. But the nose is one of the features
we commonly examine for hints of parentage. He has
already addressed his son as 'calf' and the choice of 'dam' here
for mother likewise conjures up animal breeding. He is
beginning to think that his son might not be his, and is
overwhelmed by thoughts of what is in Hermione's belly. He
wonders whether she is feeling 'affection' (in the ordinary
modern sense) for someone else. But he is also in the grip of
an 'affection' (in the early modern sense of 'emotion'), which
stabs at the core of his being, perhaps even to the extent of
giving him actual physical pain in the stomach – a common
psychosomatic phenomenon. Provided we interpret the colon
after 'unreal' in the early modern way, as a connector of
more to come, rather than a divider (see text box, p. 142), his
language indicates that he knows his emotion has no
tangible basis (is 'coactive' with the 'unreal'), and that it is like
nothing else (it 'fellow's nothing'). But it is *therefore* 'credent'
(believable), that it may 'co-join' (become a fellow) with
'something' (with a pun on 'thing' as female sexuality). In
short, he does not know why he thinks this way and yet he is
convinced she is guilty; he can feel the cuckold's horns growing
on his brows. His words thus slide from one meaning to
another, sometimes linking two very different ideas together
in an utterance that does not make syntactical sense, but
which nevertheless thereby supplies a circular and self-fulfilling
logic. The nature of his own language proves to him that
Hermione must be guilty, while proving to us that he is seriously
deranged.

PUNCTUATION

Shakespeare is sometimes difficult to read, both in the earliest printed texts and in modern editions, because of the punctuation. Early modern punctuation is not well understood, while the punctuation introduced in modern editions is often too grammatical, frequently interrupting the flow of the verse. The problem is that the same few punctuation marks are used in three distinct ways to show grammar, oratorical length of pause, and metrical structure. The most problematic of these marks is the colon, ':'. Its archetypal use is in the biblical psalms where it functions as a kind of pivot, separating the two cola or sections, which balance each other in each verse-sentence. In the sixteenth century, the colon is often used to indicate a pause in speaking, longer than a comma and shorter than a period or full stop; but it is also found in printed texts marking the ends of rhyming couplets, whether or not the sense runs on. But in all cases, it marks off a distinct but intrinsically related idea. This usage is most helpfully defined by Francis Clement in *The Petty Schole* (1587, p. 25) as a pause 'in expectation of as much more to be spoken, as is already rehearsed'. But by the beginning of the twentieth century it had come to indicate 'a discontinuity of grammatical construction' (*Oxford English Dictionary*) and today is most commonly found as the introduction of a list.

Shakespeare often writes in extended sentences of a dozen or more lines, divided into sections by colons in the early printed texts. Modern editors, however, in trying to punctuate grammatically, commonly substitute full stops or periods for one or more of these colons, using the modern semi-colon for the remainder. The effect is often to lose the momentum and connectedness of Shakespeare's sentence, so that by the time one has got to the end of the speech, one has forgotten where it began. Taking the hint offered by Clement, it is more helpful to think of the Shakespearean colon as marking an addition, or a sideways comment or digression on the main theme or flow of the sentence. The nearest modern equivalent for the latter is often the dash, although the use of that mark is usually explicitly discouraged by the general editors of modern Shakespeare series.

The actor's part

Another way that Shakespeare may have sought to influence an actor's reading was through exploiting what he knew would appear in the actor's part. Elizabethan actors were not reading full playtexts; they were reading parts containing the speeches for their character, each preceded by up to three words of cue (see p. 48). Reconstructing those parts can be revealing. Thus we see Ophelia, who is convinced that Hamlet loves her, being admonished by her brother to be careful; her father then starts harping on the same theme, but does so rather more brutally: 'Tender yourself more dearly/Or … you'll tender me a fool' (*Hamlet*, 1.3.107–9). The image is not only unsympathetic but coarse and sexual. She protests that Hamlet has behaved honourably, but this only provokes Polonius into another twenty lines that slander both her and Hamlet. It would not be surprising if she clammed up, and modern productions usually present her meek acceptance. But Ophelia's part for these twenty-four lines would look something like this:

> My lord, he hath importun'd me with love
> In honourable fashion.
>
> _____ go to.
> And hath given countenance to his speech, my lord,
> With almost all the holy vows of heaven.
>
> _____Come your ways.
> I shall obey, my lord.

There was very little time for rehearsal in the punishing schedule of Elizabethan public theatre performance. Actors would have learnt their parts in isolation, perhaps running through their lines with a partner or more experienced actor for advice on intonation and gesture. They are unlikely to have had more than a run through of each play before the performance (hence the importance of memory techniques, see p. 121). The actor playing Ophelia would not know how long Polonius's speeches were going to be. He would need to wait, listening for the cue. Here, the first Polonius speech is merely a one-line comment: 'Ay fashion you may call it, go to, go to'. An eager boy would jump in as soon as he heard the first 'go to', speaking over the second 'go to' and thereby signalling Ophelia's resistance to her father. But somewhere in the next twenty lines he has to submit. Polonius's final line might help the boy playing Ophelia manage this transition. In full it reads:

> Look to't I charge you. Come your ways.

The elision (to't) means that there are only four stresses in this line but it contains two sentences representing two distinct commands: to obey; and to follow him. It needs a pause in the middle, both to convey the idea of two different ideas and to fill up the metre. Polonius might expect her to follow after 'I charge you', but the boy is waiting for the cue 'Come your ways'. Ophelia's final line too is short, so our ears again pick up a pause or gap. Shakespeare's prosody here, combined with the likely effects on the actor of Ophelia's part, may allow us to hear tension between their characters. As a dutiful daughter, Ophelia must obey; but that does not mean she has to agree with her father's opinions, or find them fair.

Rhyming couplets

Most of Shakespeare's poetry is blank, that is, unrhymed, verse, but there are times, particularly at the end of scenes, where he uses couplets. Readers can often be uncomfortable with this practice as it seems forced and unnatural. But perhaps that is the point. We need to embrace the formality and ask what dramatic purpose it serves.

Couplets tend to be used when a character is making sententious or proverbial remarks, or summing up the action. The
couplet makes an energetic exit line, giving finality to the scene
and a sense of something different to come. An example of both
such uses occurs at the end of a scene in *2 Henry IV*, where a
discussion amongst the rebels about the likelihood of military
success against King Henry has been expressed entirely in blank
verse. The scene ends with the Archbishop of York stiffening
their resolve by conjuring up the 'fond many', the 'vulgar'
commonwealth, who had supported Henry's earlier rebellion
against Richard II, but who now regret it. They are, he suggests,
sure to win popular support:

[ARCHBISHOP:]
They that when Richard lived would have him die,
>   Are now become enamoured on his grave.
>   Thou that threw'st dust upon his goodly head,
>   ...
>   Cri'st now, 'O earth yield us that king again,
>   And take thou this.' O thoughts of men accursed!
>   'Past and to come seems best; things present, worst'.
MOWBRAY: Shall we go draw our numbers and set on?
HASTINGS: We are time's subjects, and time bids be gone.
>   (*2 Henry IV*, 1.3.101–10)

The Archbishop's proverbial and rhyming summing up (also
printed in italics in the Folio) makes their doubtful situation
seem manageable, and pushes Mowbray and Hastings into
decisive action. But Shakespeare's rhetoric simultaneously tells
another story. His audience in the public theatre may well not
have taken kindly to their forbears being accused of stupidity, or
indeed of disloyalty to the crown, by someone who is mounting
an insurrection. They are Elizabeth's subjects, not time's, and
the rhyme accursed/worst in this context undoubtedly rebounds
against the speaker.

The earlier play *Richard II* is likewise full of sententious remarks expressed in rhyming couplets, which serve to draw attention to the platitudes, encouraging us to question them. Thus, the dying John of Gaunt seeks to persuade himself and his brother York that Richard will listen to his advice:

> Where words are scarce, they are seldom spent in vain;
> For they breathe truth that breathe their words in pain.
> ...
> Though Richard my life's counsel would not hear,
> My death's sad tale may yet undeaf his ear.

> (2.1.7–16)

York does not believe him and observes that Richard's ear is 'stopped with other flattering sounds, ... Lascivious metres, to whose venom sound/The open ear of youth doth always listen' (2.1.17–20). He is right. When Richard arrives, he does not listen. He and Gaunt each try to score points through line-by-line, or stichomythic, exchanges in which words are repeated, batted to and fro between them. Gaunt occasionally tries to trump Richard by rhyming with him, but Richard refuses to rhyme and uses the stichomythia to wriggle away from Gaunt's accusations. This old technique, common in classical and classically inspired plays, underscores the futility of their argument.

> [GAUNT:] Since thou does seek to kill my name in me,
>   I mock my name great king to flatter thee.
> RICHARD: Should dying men flatter with those that live?
> GAUNT: No, no, men living flatter those that die.
> RICHARD: Thou now a-dying sayst thou flatt'rest me.
> GAUNT: O no: thou diest, though I the sicker be.

> (2.1.86–91)

Another battle of rhymes takes place in *Othello*. The duke needs Othello to go and fight the Turks. If it makes him happy to take Brabantio's daughter with him, he has no intention of stopping him. His remarks to the outraged father take the form of rhyming commonplaces which are intended to be soothing:

> When remedies are past, the griefs are ended
> By seeing the worst, which late on hopes depended.
> To mourn a mischief that is past and gone
> Is the next way to draw new mischief on.
> ...
> The robbed that smiles steals something from the thief;
> He robs himself that spends a bootless grief.
>
> (1.3.201–9)

Brabantio is incensed and replies scornfully in the same register, but reduced to absurdity:

> So let the Turk of Cyprus us beguile:
> We lose it not so long as we can smile.

And so on for another eight lines, stressing that such old saws are meaningless:

> These sentences, to sugar or to gall,
> Being strong on both sides, are equivocal.
>
> (1.3.210–17)

The Duke seems to take his point, without changing his mind about the conduct of the war. Normally a verse speaker, he turns to Othello to give his orders in prose. His warning that Othello must 'slubber the gloss' of his new fortunes is not complimentary, since 'slubber' means soil, stain, or darken. He has clearly had enough of all this trivial, domestic nonsense.

Case study: *A Midsummer Night's Dream*

Written in the mid-1590s, *A Midsummer Night's Dream* has characters that include a legendary hero of ancient Athens and his mythical Amazonian queen; a set of mismatched aristocratic lovers; and some very English tradesmen, who rehearse and perform an old-fashioned melodrama with variable vocal and intellectual expertise. In the forest, these characters are mirrored by a hierarchy of fairies and sprites, who sing songs, weave spells, and bicker amongst themselves.

The play incorporates a particularly wide range of styles in both verse and prose, which are shared across social divides – and even species – to a range of comic effects. The iambic pentameters can appear as blank verse, rhyming couplets, and alternately rhyming lines; the fairies can use any of those forms but also employ seven- or eight-syllable, four-stress lines when engaged in particularly fairy activities.

The tradesmen's play varies from alternately rhymed iambic pentameter to alternate lines of eight and six syllables with internal rhymes and alliteration – like traditional ballads. The tradesmen themselves usually speak in prose but in moments of stress or of revelation their language can become either highly patterned or non-verbal. The musical world of the play is equally varied: fairy song; hunting horns; players' trumpet; fairy music 'such as charmeth sleep'; and fairy evocation of rural music, including, in the Folio text of the play, the tongs and the bones.

When Bottom the weaver is magicked into wearing an ass's head, his fellows run away terrified. To give himself courage, he stomps up and down, singing, which wakes the fairy queen who has been sleeping nearby. There are several opportunities for his performance to incorporate the sound of a donkey braying – first in the refrain to his song 'And dares not answer nay' (neigh) (3.1.122). Later, after Titania's observation that the watery eye of the moon appears to be causing the very flowers to weep, 'Lamenting some enforced chastity', there needs to be some non-verbal, probably donkey-like or other rutting sound from him to prompt her instruction, 'Tie up my love's tongue, bring him silently' (183–6) – the authority of her remark suggesting that it is not her chastity that is under threat, but his. Far from the pretty floweriness of Victorian performances and illustrations of these scenes, Bottom as ass introduces an overt, noisy, but unspoken sexuality.

When he wakes from his 'dream' which has already faded even as he tries to grasp the memory of having slept with the fairy queen, he tells us: 'I have had a dream past the wit of man to say what dream it was … Methought I was – there is no man can tell what. Methought I was, and methought I had. But man is but a patch'd fool, if he will offer to say what methought I had' (4.1.203–10). More decorous productions simply have him gesture to his head where his long ears had been, but this dim grasping after another identity gets funnier if the thought of what he was – the ass with long ears – leads to the thought of having been the possessor of that other proverbially long part of an ass's anatomy. Size matters, after all.

In a mixture of awe and pride, he expresses this dimly remembered transcendent experience in a rhetorically patterned but absurdly muddled paraphrase of St Paul's first letter to the Corinthians in its Geneva bible translation. Paul is attempting to explain the mystery of God, 'which none of the princes of this world hath known … things which eye hath not seen, neither ear hath heard … For what man knoweth the things of a man save the spirit of man, which is in him?' (1 Corinthians, 2.8–11). Shakespeare's borrowings here are part of the characterisation of the play; many weavers in England at that time were exiled French Protestant Huguenots, and this parody of a particularly Protestant translation of the bible cannot be accidental. Bottom's dream is a mystery of the body jumbled to signify more than itself as the man strives to find the ass within him: 'The eye of man hath not heard, the ear of man hath not seen, man's hand is not able to taste, his tongue to conceive, nor his heart to report, what my dream was' (4.1.210–14).

Shakespeare also creates a sense of both character and unspoken meaning through the way in which he varies the same basic metrical form between speakers from the same social class. The play opens with Theseus, duke of Athens, addressing his bride to be, the Amazonian Queen Hippolyta:

> Now, fair Hippolyta, our nuptial hour
> Draws on apace; four happy days bring in
> Another moon; but oh, methinks, how slow
> This old moon wanes. She lingers my desires,
> Like to a step-dame or a dowager,
> Long withering out a young man's revenue.
>
> (1.1.1–6)

The speech begins insistently, with consecutive stresses on 'now' and 'fair'. This is useful for an opening line; the actor needs to calm the audience and control the stage, since there is no stage lighting to help him on an Elizabethan stage. But Theseus is impatient for his wedding night, and as we know from our own experience, and saw in the last chapter (p. 94), anticipation can make the time drag. Accordingly, lines 3 and 4 incorporate a succession of long vowel sounds. Although these lines can be spoken in a regular de dum, de dum iambic rhythm, they cannot effectively be performed that way. The sense and the writing both demand that the speaker linger on (and inevitably stress) the syllables 'moon', 'oh', 'how slow', 'old moon wanes', 'ling-', '-sires'. Even the syllable 'thinks' is long, despite its short vowel, because of its multiple consonants.

There are a number of different poetic techniques at work in these lines. A line-length in poetry is itself a form of punctuation, grouping words together in an idea, and causing a short hiatus at the end, even when the sense runs on. A word at the end of a line is therefore in a very strong position; a good speaker will let it hang in the air while maintaining the forward momentum of the sentence. The combination of words 'how slow' (line 3), with two consecutive long syllables, is slow in itself, but positioned at the end of the line, as here, they encourage the speaker to linger even longer, even though the line is enjambed (i.e. run into the next). These stretched, slow syllables, combined with the enjambment, provide a sense of arching momentum – like falling off a cliff. In the next line, a different stretching technique is at work: the combination 'moon wanes' is a bit of a tongue twister if spoken aloud quickly, because the similar mouth shapes required to pronounce 'oo' and 'w' are interrupted by the different tongue position for 'n' and followed by the opposite mouth shape for the 'a' sound in wanes. When Shakespearean phrases are physically difficult to say, it is usually an indication that the actor should not rush them.

It is not that the speaker needs to slow down; far from it. He needs to be aware of the continuing steady iambic pentameter metre and keep to time, else the pace of the delivery will be lost and we will be bored. But he also needs to identify the stresses that will bring out the sense. This will inevitably result in the compression of certain other syllables, and sometimes too the introduction of slight pauses. Such pauses might correspond with the punctuation, but since punctuation is often merely grammatical, they will not inevitably do so.

In the passage below, pauses introduced around the surprising reference in this context to the step-dame and the dowager would allow Hippolyta to register, and us to hear, a joke to which she, as a former devotress to Diana, chaste huntress and moon goddess, will not take kindly. He states that the old crone moon has been preventing him from claiming what he regards as his rightful inheritance. Hippolyta, however, is only too aware that she is his prize in both monetary and sexual terms.

A good performer will find a rhythm in these lines which might also accommodate non-verbal sounds (laughs, grunts, groans for example) as well as space for gestures, and which pulls against the underlying iambic pentameter metre, while also keeping in time with it. While each performance will be individual to a particular speaker, and may also vary in the same speaker from performance to performance, there might be as many as six stressed syllables in line 3, and two pauses in line 5, perhaps accommodated by compressing 'dowager' to two syllables (dow-ger) as suggested here:

Now, fair Hippolyta, our nuptial hour

Draws on apace; four happy days bring in

Another moon, but oh, methinks, how slow

This old moon wanes.   She lingers my desires

Like to a step-dame   or a dowager

Long withering out a young man's revenue.

I emphasise that this is not the only way to deliver these lines; but one thing is certain, they are not de dum, de dum, de dum.

TIPS ON READING SHAKESPEARE

1. Read out loud.
2. Notice which syllables need to be stressed in order to bring out the shape and sense of the sentence and the line. How does this play with the underlying metre?
3. Do not be fazed by contractions such as i'th' for 'in the'. For example, in 'To lose't or give't away' (*Othello*, 3.4.67), say 'it' both times, but quickly so as to maintain the metre.
4. Take notice when a combination of words is physically difficult to say. Don't rush it.

TIPS ON READING SHAKESPEARE (*cont.*)

5. Pay attention to the end of the line. Is it endstopped, or is it enjambed (run into the next)? What word is in the final position? Why might it be significant?

6. How are passages and lines shared between speakers? Are the speakers playing ball with each other? Or are they digging in their heels?

7. Which words are connected by rhyme, alliteration (beginning with the same letter), or assonance (containing a similar vowel sound)? How does this contribute to the pattern of the line and also to the sense?

8. Keep up the pace; be alive to potential pauses created by the rhetoric, but accommodate these within the tempo of the line, so as to maintain the shape and coherence of the sentence. This makes it easier to hear and understand.

Hippolyta's response is literally more measured, with important words coinciding more exactly with the iambic pentameter metre:

> Four days will quickly steep themselves in night,
> Four nights will quickly dream away the time,
> And then the moon, like to a silver bow,
> New bent in heaven, shall behold the night
> Of our solemnities.

$$(1.1.7–11)$$

But there is a small hiatus in her third line. The metre would demand a stress on the word 'to'. Meaning demands a stress on 'like' instead, which creates a tiny pause after 'moon', where indeed the grammar too demands a comma. It is a wistful moment. Did she, when she was still an Amazonian queen and not, as now, a captive prize of war, once wield a bow with silver mounts? She does not say; nor does she say what she thinks about her impending marriage. But we might know that Amazons never married, and we might suppose that the moon, now again in the character of the crescent moon, Diana, the huntress with a bow, not the old crone, might 'behold' the ceremony with regret. As we have seen, Titania, Hippolyta's counterpart in the fairy world, will later also detect some sadness in the moon.

Theseus then admits:

> Hippolyta, I wooed thee with my sword,
> And won thy love doing thee injuries,
> But I will wed thee in another key,
> With pomp, with triumph, and with revelling.
>
> (1.1.16–19)

Theseus's language here is likewise measured; perhaps it is the measure of confidence, although it seems both an acknowledgement and a solemn promise. She does not reply, but silence on stage can speak volumes. Wedding is one thing, marriage quite another.

The theme of forced marriage now continues in another key, as Egeus enters with his daughter Hermia and her two lovers, Lysander and Demetrius. The verse form is the same, iambic pentameter blank verse, but now, Shakespeare's use of rhetoric and rhythm creates an impression of frustrated and impatient old age. It is full of repetitions and reiterations, and insists on his rights as a father. The accusation that Egeus makes against Lysander that he has bewitched his daughter anticipates that which Desdemona's father Brabantio makes against black Othello in the later play. It is a serious charge, and in performance, Lysander might well start to object, but Egeus cuts off any denial by launching into a catalogue of his frivolous love-gifts and, as Shakespeare mischievously writes, complaining about his 'feigned' poetry. Here, in modernised spelling, is the text of this speech as it appears in both Folio and Quarto:

Full of vexation, come I with complaint
Against my child, my daughter Hermia.
                    Stand forth Demetrius.

My noble lord,
This man hath my consent to marry her.
                    Stand forth Lysander

And my gracious duke,
This man hath bewitched the bosom of my child.
Thou, thou, Lysander, thou hast given her rhymes,
And interchang'd love tokens with my child;
Thou hast by moonlight at her window sung,
With faining voice, verses of feigning love,
And stolen the impression of her fantasy
With bracelets of thy hair, rings, gauds, conceits,
Knacks, trifles, nosegays, sweetmeats – messengers
Of strong prevailments in unhardened youth.
With cunning hast thou filch'd my daughter's heart,
Turned her obedience (which is due to me)
To stubborn harshness.

                                    (1.1.22–38)

Most modern editions of this play, however, follow an emendation first made by Nicholas Rowe in 1709 and print the italicized sentences in the passage above as if they were part of Egeus's speech:

Stand forth, Demetrius. My noble lord,
This man hath my consent to marry her.
Stand forth, Lysander. And my gracious duke,
This man hath bewitch'd the bosom of my child …

These now spoken commands to 'Stand forth' are imperious and have the effect of obscuring the beautifully observed fussiness in the rest of Egeus's speech.

Treated as stage directions, the verb 'stand' should be understood as the transitive verb, that is instructing Egeus to bring Demetrius and Lysander to the attention of the Duke. This provides scope for some comic action, which would greatly enhance audience memory as to which of the two otherwise almost identical young men is the one that Egeus favours. He might, for instance, draw Demetrius forward or display him proudly in some way, but push Lysander. Whatever he does, the empty half line would be taken up in action.

Egeus now demands the ancient Athenian right to dispose his daughter as he sees fit: to marriage or, if she does not agree with his choice, to death, or to life as a nun. Theseus, who has subdued Hippolyta by violence, is the upholder of Athenian law, and in very measured tones tells Hermia to 'be advised' and obey. He turns her rhetoric back on itself, interrupting its regular series of unstress/stress, with the sharp contradiction of stress/unstress in the word 'Rather', before reverting to regularity:

HERMIA: I would my father looked but with my eyes.

THESEUS: Rather, your eyes must with his judgement look.

He also turns the image she uses into its reverse. She wishes her father understood her partiality; Theseus urges the renaissance ideal of the eyes as gateways to the mind and the understanding. But his line also puns on 'judgement' as legal decision, after which he then reiterates the law.

All this while, Hippolyta stands by, silent. Theseus draws attention to what might well be her dismay at this scene by asking her 'What cheer my love?' She does not reply, but modern actors invariably make use of that silence to express her displeasure. Silent characters can often be invisible when one is reading, but they can be made to be the focus of attention on stage.

Reading silence

There are so many words in Shakespeare that it is easy to forget that sound needs to be set against silence in order to become meaningful. Silence is particularly difficult for the silent reader to 'read' and to 'hear'. We have seen how small silences might be written in to the verse. Longer periods of silence, however, would need a stage direction. There is one instance in *The Winter's Tale* (3.2.10), where the word 'Silence' is written in italics and ranged to the right – the same position and typeface as the italicised sentences in *Dream* examined above. Again, it is surely a stage direction; an instruction to the company to keep an awed silence as Hermione walks in for her trial. Unfortunately, it is most often presented in modern editions as an order spoken by the officer of the court, demanding an excitable hubbub from the crowd for him to quell – exactly the opposite effect from the one Shakespeare probably wrote.

At the end of that play, after being thought to be dead for sixteen years, Hermione has to maintain absolute silence and stillness in the form of a statue, albeit a statue that looks as if it is both about to move and to speak. The 'bringing to life' of this statue is accomplished as characters speak over instrumental music, an almost invariably powerful emotional effect, and Hermione walks towards her husband in the mirror image of her walk into court in the earlier scene. She is then described by Polixenes and Camillo as embracing Leontes, hanging round his neck. She does not speak to him, however, although she does speak to her long lost daughter. Shakespeare thus leaves it up to us to imagine her feelings for the husband whose jealousy has caused her so much pain. We do not know whether her embrace expresses joy and love, or resignation and sorrow, or a complex mix of conflicting feelings. This is the power of silence.

A profound use of silence also occurs in a family reunion in *Coriolanus*. Coriolanus, who has been exiled from Rome and is now leading an attack on the city at the head of the Volscian armys, is approached by his mother, wife, and child, and their female friend, who have come to plead with him to give up his attack. Volumnia, his mother, who has brought him up to be a warrior and killing machine, speaks at some length, and ends by scorning his lack of family feeling. Her speech is followed by the stage direction '*He holds her by the hand, silent*' (5.3.182). This denotes a pause much longer than can be written into the verse. It can in fact be made to last for twenty seconds or more – an age in stage time – and is perhaps a reminder to the prompter not to interrupt. It is an extraordinary moment. He knows that if he accedes to her request, he will be killed by the Volsces. But we do not know whether Volumnia realises this.

Earlier in the scene, Coriolanus has stood watching while his family walks on stage. He tells us the order in which the characters enter and the gestures they employ: his mother is holding his son by the hand; she bows 'As if Olympus to a molehill should/In supplication nod', while the child has an 'aspect of intercession which/Great nature cries 'Deny not'' (5.3.22–33). It is a small, vulnerable family group of women and a boy, although he describes it in terms of great natural forces. He is clearly moved, but tries to banish his feelings. He does not care, he says, if the Volsces destroy Italy:

> I'll never
> Be such a gosling to obey instinct, but stand
> As if a man were author of himself
> And knew no other kin.

His wife then addresses him, 'My lord and husband', which introduces the following exchange, given here with modern spelling but with the Folio's lineation and punctuation:

> CORIOLANUS: These eyes are not the same I wore in Rome.
> VIRGILIA: The sorrow that delivers us thus chang'd,

> Makes you think so.
> CORIOLANUS: Like a dull actor now, I have forgot my part,
> And I am out, even to a full disgrace. Best of my flesh,
> Forgive my tyranny: but do not say
> For that forgive our Romans.
>
> (5.3.38–44)

The third line here is short, while the fifth contains fifteen syllables. The passage is usually relineated into seven, more or less
regular ten-syllable pentameter lines in modern editions. But F's
lineation has more interesting possibilities: Virgilia's incomplete
line allows a silence in which Coriolanus can be painfully lost for
words – a contrast to his previous description of *her* as 'my
gracious silence' (2.1.166). The image of an actor who has
'dried' is taken direct from embarrassing playhouse experience,
and Shakespeare has provided an agitated rhythm, with consecutive stresses on 'dull actor'. This aside to himself takes up a full
two lines, which suggests that 'Best of my flesh' should be in a
line on its own, both belatedly balancing her previous half
line and providing more silent time as he struggles to regain
his composure and find the words. The excruciating silence
between husband and wife is necessary; they both know his
actions have endangered his family, and in the Folio text the
word 'tyranny' is accentuated by a slight oratorical pause
indicated by the colon (usually changed to a comma in modern
editions). He is not denying the nature of his action.
Shakespeare's most emotional, psychologically compelling
moments are sometimes written in the gaps of his verse – if only
we can see, and hear them.

5

Interpreting Shakespeare

'how easy is a bush supposed a bear'
(*A Midsummer Night's Dream*, 5.1.22)

This book has tried to show that the difficulties we commonly experience when reading Shakespeare are a necessary part of the writing and construction of his work. The characters in his plays each have a slightly different take on their play's central ethical problem, while the speakers in his poems have to contend with the humour of the narrator or with the very structure of the verse itself. Shakespeare never supplies any single or straightforward moral answer to the problems he poses. Instead the multiple points of view in each of his works create complexity that engages our imaginations, and invites response, allowing us to make connections between his work and social, cultural, or historical moments that he cannot have foreseen.

Such connections are an essential part of performance. Most books about Shakespeare necessarily involve historical enquiry: what could this word, this image, this idea, signify at the time Shakespeare was writing? And just as important, what did it not mean? But performance demands something more: it involves a set of actors relating directly to their audience; one can only ever perform in the present. Shakespeare's plays were popular when he wrote them because they engaged their audiences on all levels, physically and emotionally, as well as intellectually. All directors of Shakespeare productions will be trying to give modern audiences a similar all-round, intellectually and emotionally engaged experience. They will probably also aspire to be new and innovative. But the very best interpretations now, whether within the pages of a critical book or on the boards of a stage, will result when immediate modern relevancy proceeds from a profound engagement with the structure of the text. How does the interface between play, performer, and audience work? And is it possible to develop ways of judging the relative validity of different interpretations, or is it all simply a 'matter of opinion'?

This chapter consists of case studies of three plays that have proved highly controversial in modern times, and considers how they have been reinterpreted, represented, and even restructured – in some cases from the very moment Shakespeare first wrote them. Throughout the twentieth century, *The Taming of the Shrew* was one of his most frequently performed plays, yet recently there have been calls for it to be left firmly on the shelf for being too misogynistic; *The Merchant of Venice* seems to some impossible to perform in the wake of Nazi anti-Semitism. I shall begin, however, with *Henry V*, which has been used as a *critique* on the wars in the Falklands and Iraq; by the US military as an *exemplum* for soldiers going to Iraq and Afghanistan; and as a training manual for business leaders. How can this be? Clearly much more could be said about each of these plays than I have space for here, so my aim is to offer some principles which readers can then apply to other productions and other plays.

Henry V and the wooden O

Earlier, we met John Davies of Hereford leaning on a pillar in the middle gallery at a public theatre and ascribing a clear moral and social value to the experience (p. xiv). By contrast, Shakespeare's more famous and much grander evocation of the 'wooden O' in the opening Chorus to *Henry V* is, on close inspection, both slippery and ambiguous:

> O for a muse of fire, that would ascend
> The brightest heaven of invention:
> A kingdom for a stage, princes to act,
> And monarchs to behold the swelling scene.
> Then should the warlike Harry, like himself
> Assume the port of Mars, and at his heels,
> Leashed in like hounds, should famine, sword, and fire
> Crouch for employment. But pardon, gentles all,
> The flat unraisèd spirits that hath dared
> On this unworthy scaffold to bring forth
> So great an object. Can this cockpit hold
> The vasty fields of France? Or may we cram
> Within this wooden O the very casques
> That did affright the air at Agincourt?
>
> (*Henry V*, Chorus 1, lines 1–14)

Provided one knows that Mars is god of war, and 'muse' a source of inspiration for poetry, there are only two words in these lines that are likely to cause any difficulty for a modern audience: 'port' means 'deportment' or carriage, particularly 'stately bearing'; 'casques' are helmets. 'Vasty' (i.e. vast) is unusual, but self-evident; Shakespeare may have invented that form of the word, and it was not much taken up by other writers. He used it three times in this play, and once in both *Henry IV* and *The Merchant of Venice*. In each case, it signifies something huge, wild, unknown, or terrifying – death's jaws, the ocean, the wilds of Arabia or of central Asia.

Putting the words together, however, is probably not meant to be easy. The speech deals with the thorny issue of realism in art, and also deftly pokes fun at the common moral objection to actors dressing up as their betters. If we are to comprehend it, we need to explore both its intellectual context and its emotional structure. It is over the top from that first word, or rather sound, 'Oh'. The Chorus demands not just a muse, but a muse of fire. Prior to the discovery by Nicolaus Copernicus (1473–1543) that the earth revolved around the sun, fire was thought to occupy a space between earth and heaven. This muse, however, must enable the author to reach into the 'highest heaven', which turns out to be the space within himself, his own imagination. Shakespeare then takes the concept of all the world being a stage and turns it inside out: this stage would need to be a kingdom in order to do justice to this story about a historical king of England; nay, more than a single kingdom, a world, for there would have to be multiple princes for actors, and monarchs for audience. Later, however, he addresses the audience as 'gentles all'. This democratisation is a diminution in rank from the hyperbolic request for an audience of monarchs, yet it might still cause an Elizabethan un-gentle groundling a slight chuckle, while subtly demoting any aristocrat in the lord's room. In reality of course, the actors were at best servants of a great lord. Some would be no more than hired hands, servants of servants, while the audience consisted of a complete cross-section of the local populace, arranged, as we have seen, according to class.

Such discrepancy between the rhetoric and the reality is the clue that we need to be on our guard with this play. So if, ideally, we would need to have a prince acting a king, acting a god, how would *Harry* be 'like' himself? What kind of 'imitation' would that be? Who or what is Harry in that instance? Conversely, since we do not have princes for actors, can the representation of Harry be 'like' Harry at all, let alone Harry as god? If to be like himself Harry has to stride across the world with the dogs of war at his heels ready to unleash famine, death, and desecration on the world, what would that mean for us, the un-gentle, who usually suffer more than the wealthy in times of war?

The Chorus clearly finds this image glorious but then he asks pardon. For what? The apology hangs at the end of the line, and in the Folio there is a colon signalling both pause and more to come. The gap might just give us time to reflect back on the terror that kings as gods can impose on the rest of us. But of course, the next line tells us he is not apologising for war but for the fact that there are no princes, no raising the spirits of the dead, only common actors, and a rough scaffold stage. It is up to us, he says, to supply the glory in our imagination: the huge open fields of France, and the two opposing armies, all decked out in helmets that sparkle in the air. In asking us to do that, he has made us complicit in a deceit that goes way beyond theatre. Apart from anything else, armies are never adequately equipped; those serving in early modern armies would have provided their own armour and the ordinary foot soldier would at most have had a buff leather coat; no glittering 'casque' for him. People in Shakespeare's first audiences would have known that. Some might themselves have returned only recently from fighting as members of the private armies authorised by Elizabeth to support the Protestant cause in the wars of religion in France, or the revolt against Spanish rule in the Netherlands. Some of those returning soldiers had been dumped at Dover with no money to get home. The queen had issued an order, condemning the disorder that had erupted and forbidding them to sell their arms. War is only ever glorious in official propaganda. This speech is therefore complex for a reason. It is written this way in order to underscore that the Chorus is peddling a fiction. This is going to be a play that will ask us hard questions about judgement and justice in war and government.

Of course, no spectator would have the time to unpack this speech in any detail as the lines flash past in performance. But phrase-by-phrase translation is not how we engage with language in the theatre. There, we pick up information as much through tone of voice, gesture, and costuming as we do through the sense of the words. The rather staid rhythms and the function of the Chorus as authority figure encourages companies to cast a mature actor in the part, someone who can summon gravitas, but it is not a leading role and will not be taken by the star. If we were regular visitors to Shakespeare's theatre, we would know who the stars were, and this actor would not be one of them; we might be impatient for him to get off and let the star come on. The succession of grand images would encourage him to adopt an authoritative posture and gesture, but the deferential tone he adopts towards us the audience might amuse us, while his poeticisms and his reminders that there will be a gap between what he wants us to see and what we do see, reinforce the idea of fiction.

The character of Henry in this play is a master of morale-boosting rhetoric; commanders faced with trying to get their troops 'unto the breach' (3.1.1) need to employ stirring words. His phrases have been borrowed by countless political, military, and business leaders for their own purposes, while 'band of brothers' (4.3.60) became the title of a TV mini-series about a company of American soldiers fighting in France in World War II. But Henry's exhortations do not stand unchallenged in the play as a whole, which in its Folio version continually undercuts these heroic certainties. The first scene in the Folio (but not the Quarto) begins with two leading bishops in the English church, plotting to encourage the king to go to war merely to distract him from his plan to sequester church funds. The whole of England in this play seethes with intrigues and petty jealousies. The second Chorus introduces the discovery of a plot against Henry by a group of noblemen. The second scene shows a quarrel over a woman amongst a raggle-taggle group of Londoners – including a boy, and a whore and three common soldiers from the *Henry IV* plays. Those characters are similarly out for what they can get, but their misdemeanours pale in comparison with those of their betters. They then lament the death of their friend, the fat knight, Falstaff, one of the most popular characters Shakespeare ever created, and a mass of contradictions in himself. He had been a companion to the young Henry in his wild days, but he hides from the battle against the rebels at the end of the first part of *Henry IV*. He is a coward; yet his words suggest that there needs to be a better reason for going to war than the pursuit of honour:

> Can honour set to a leg? No. Or an arm? No. Or take away the grief of a wound? No ... What is honour? A word. What is in that word? Honour. What is that honour? Air.
>
> (*1 Henry IV*, 5.1.132–7)

The second part of *Henry IV* has much the same trajectory as the first part, repeating its scenic structure, but in a darker vein. Falstaff corruptly (yet humorously) exploits his position as king's recruiting officer, and assumes he will be made Lord Chief Justice as soon as Henry inherits the crown; his aim is to pervert justice, and line his own pockets. Instead, Henry disowns him, and casts him off. He is right to do so, yet this action is also a betrayal of friendship. There is repeated reference to this event and the intractable moral conflict it represents throughout the play of *Henry V*, and generations of readers, play-goers, and critics have blamed Henry for his lack of loyalty to his friend. The Welsh soldier Fluellen, however, comparing Henry with Alexander the Great, excuses him:

> Alexander killed his friend Clytus, being in his ales and his cups; so also Harry Monmouth being in his right wits, and his good judgements, turned away the fat knight ... I have forgot his name.
>
> (*Henry V*, 4.7.42–8)

Fluellen's comment, with its telling grammatical confusion in the phrase 'so also' to introduce an idea that is both comparison *and* contrast, comes immediately after Henry has ordered the killing of the French prisoners. Was that act against the law of war? What we saw might qualify as a war crime: an order given in cold blood albeit under the threat of imminent attack. Fluellen has heard otherwise, however, and is confident that it was a justifiable retribution for the French sacking of the English baggage train and the wholesale slaughter of the boys who had been gathered there for safety. In every scene, this play thus dramatises the confusion and 'fog of war', as well as the ways in which the concept of just war, both in the conduct of engagement, and in the rationale for going to war in the first place, can be manipulated.

In the theatre, where two whole armies are represented by a few men and 'four or five most vile and ragged foils' (*Henry V*, Chorus, Act 4), such contradictions are kept before our eyes. In Laurence Olivier's beautiful film of the play, by contrast, the theatrically made-up actors, and the film-set representation of a bare Elizabethan stage melt before our eyes into a picture book seascape of little boats, or a lush green French countryside, and a heroic representation of Henry himself. The settings of some of these scenes are far from realistic; some are based on the illustrations in the late fifteenth-century book of hours belonging to the Duc de Berri. Thus the film's structure and visual qualities maintain the sense of a fiction that I have been describing, but the presentation ensures that we see the action through the Chorus's eyes, rather than being left to use our own. In the film, the imagining is done for us, and the contradictions thereby levelled out.

The text used in Olivier's film was also judiciously pruned, streamlining the dialogue in which Henry in disguise talks to three common soldiers, John Bates, Alexander Court, and Michael Williams, and thereby neutralising Williams's criticism of the war by giving him Bates's line in which he promises to fight 'lustily'. In the Folio Williams remains confused, unable quite to see how Henry has managed to deflect his doubts

(4.1.86–227). Sometimes, meaning can be changed simply by reassigning the dialogue. The film also omits the stark brutalities of Henry's speech before the town of Harfleur, which threatens the citizens with rape, pillage, and murder if they do not surrender (3.3). A sixteenth-century audience would have known that this speech was no empty rhetoric. The rules of engagement, based on instructions to the Israelites set out in the bible (Deuteronomy 20.10–14), allowed a victorious army to sack a town if it had forced a siege by holding out against them. But the Duke of Alva, in attempting to crush the revolt against Spanish rule in the Netherlands, had recently sacked a succession of towns, whether or not they had resisted – events regarded as some of the worst atrocities in history until overtaken by the excesses of twentieth-century war.

Both visually and textually, therefore, Olivier's film removes an entire level of perception and makes simple and heroic something that the Folio text of the play presents as complex and problematic. Olivier knew that he had to produce a patriotic film – part of the war effort against Nazi Germany. He loathed what he saw as the war-mongering brutal aspect of Henry's character, and his alterations were consciously designed to make the character more palatable. Perhaps that was understandable given the historical moment in which the film was produced. But similar cuts and rearrangements occur in the Quarto text too. It seems that people have always wanted to remove the play's uncomfortable qualities, and make it simply heroic. The Folio text is much more interesting than that.

The Taming of the Shrew

The taming of a shrewish woman is a stock motif in folk stories and ballads from all over Europe and merges into the modern romantic novel theme of woman submitting to a masterful lover. Thus the *Coventry Evening Telegraph* enthusiastically described Peggy Ashcroft's performance as Kate in John Barton's production:

> Long before she is wholly tamed, Miss Ashcroft gives the impression that she is not minding her rough treatment so very much. As she walks off after Petruchio has baited her with the new dress and hat, a smile of submission lights up her face. It is a delightful touch.
>
> (22 June 1960)

It is this kind of reaction to a romanticising performance tradition that has (rightly) enraged modern feminist critics.

Shakespeare's play, however, begins not with the story of Kate and Petruchio, but in the middle of a violent argument between a drunken man and the hostess of a pub:

> SLY: I'll feeze you, in faith.
> HOSTESS: A pair of stocks, you rogue!
> SLY: Y'are a baggage, the Slys are no rogues. Look in the chronicles; we came in with Richard Conqueror.

The hostess goes to fetch an officer and Sly falls asleep but immediately a genuine representative of the upper classes who may or may not have come in with William the Conqueror enters from his idle pursuit of hunting. He too has an inflated sense of his own importance, demonstrated by his refusal to listen to expert advice. Not content with giving his huntsman basic orders to 'tender well my hounds', he flatly contradicts the man's detailed observations of the dog Belman's hunting performance with 'Thou art a fool. If Echo were as fleet/I would esteem him worth a dozen such' (Scene 1.14–27). Since, by his own admission, Echo is not as fleet, the proposition falls.

So far, we have seen nothing of what judging from its title and several centuries of criticism this play is supposed to be about – the subjugation of women. On the contrary we have seen a capable businesswoman who is quite aware of her rights, and her social counterpart the huntsman, both standing up to the arrogance of those who see themselves in authority over them. We have also been introduced to a concept and a linguistic device both of which are going to assume structural importance for this play: an argument predicated on the word 'If'. There is 'much virtue in "if"' as Touchstone, one of Shakespeare's wise fools, points out (*As You Like It*, 5.4.97).

The Folio marks the opening scene as usual, '*Actus primus. Scaena Prima*', but most modern editions follow the eighteenth-century critic and poet Alexander Pope in labelling it as the first of two 'Induction' scenes. This is a small change, perhaps, and certainly not in itself apparent to those watching in the theatre, but it has had a significant critical effect. It encourages the idea that this is not the play proper, that the two scenes can effectively be ignored in any detailed discussion, or cut from performances. True, they do not get on very fast with the shrew-taming story, but as with any other opening scene in Shakespeare, they provide us with an essential critical perspective. They tell us how to read the play.

The Lord decides to have some fun. He gets his servants to take Sly and dress him in fine clothes. When he wakes they are to tell him that he has been ill and that 'he is nothing but a mighty lord'. Trumpets are heard. The lord is excited – trumpets are always stirring things – and sends to see who it is. Confidently, and wrongly as usual, he anticipates the answer, deciding that they must be heralding the imminent arrival of 'some noble gentleman'. Instead, in walks a company of players. It is a beautifully observed joke right down to the Lord's inability to remember the name of the actor he has previously seen playing the romantic lead while, true to form, pronouncing on his ability. It must have given Shakespeare some enjoyment to write it.

> This fellow I remember
> Since once he played a farmer's eldest son;
> 'Twas where you woo'd the gentlewoman so well.
> I have forgot your name, but sure that part
> Was aptly fitted, and naturally performed.
>
> (Scene 1.81–5)

The Lord may have forgotten his name, but we, unusually, do know which of Shakespeare's actors was playing the part since the Folio prints the name Sincklo as a speech prefix. This was the hired man, John Sincler. From what we can piece together about this man, the romantic lead would *not* be 'aptly fitted' type-casting. Indeed a contemporary audience would be more used to seeing his lean little body portraying minor and rather crabbed characters; it is thought he played the apothecary in *Romeo and Juliet*. The in-joke could have been considerable.

The Lord continues with his ruse – and Shakespeare continues with his presentation of a sophisticated theory of drama. The Lord anticipates that Sly in his new role as 'lord' will not know how to behave while watching a play and warns the players not to laugh at him, for if they 'should smile, he grows impatient' (Scene 1.97). Sly will inevitably become confused as to which of his two roles (the lord or the beggar) is real. While sliding between identities, he will be unwittingly acting the designated role 'mad lord'. The stage actors will be unaware that while performing their play they will be both watching and performing in the Lord's play. The 'real' Lord, on the other hand, will knowingly be both a spectator of his own handiwork and an actor in it since he is to be dressed as a serving man and has instructed his actual servants to act towards him accordingly. But he, like all the other 'real-life' characters in Shakespeare's play, is also an *unwitting* actor. None of them knows that *we* are watching. It's beginning to be quite difficult to know where 'reality' lies.

The theatricality of the opening sets up an intellectual framework for understanding the old tale, the taming play. Shakespeare's play has several marked transitions of register. There is the naturalism of the drunken brawl; then the theatrical theory underlying the lord's scene; and then some markedly old-fashioned diction as the taming play – here in fact a play-within-the-play – gets underway (Scene 3, or Act 1.1.1–45). As Sly disappears from view, the play situation gets forgotten and Shakespeare's language becomes more his own. But in drawing us in, Shakespeare also implicates us. The violent elements in the story he presents, though set in Padua, were legally possible in his society. They still do occur within marriages in Britain – wife battering knows no social or ethnic boundaries.

I said earlier that the play's conscious theatricality is a structural principle creating a sense of the idea 'If'. And it is a silent 'If' that underpins Kate's final speech:

> Thy husband is thy lord, thy life, thy keeper,
> Thy head, thy sovereign; one that cares for thee,
> And for thy maintenance commits his body
> To painful labour both by sea and land,
> To watch the night in storms, the day in cold,
> Whilst thou liest warm at home, secure and safe;
>
> (5.2.146–51)

If husbands really did such things, there would at least be grounds for a bargain. But of course, none of the husbands on stage at that moment has behaved that way, and we have seen Kate far from home, neither warm nor safe. We have also seen her learn how to manipulate her husband, getting her own way in important practical matters, simply by agreeing with him when he says that day is night, and the sun is the moon (5.5.1–25). In a situation of inequality, that is how a woman is forced to manage a difficult husband if she does not want to become the saucepan-wielding scold of the Stratford misericord (p. 110).

Shakespeare's play pattern, with its insistence on acting, seems to be asking who has tamed whom. It ends still within the fantasy play-within-the-play, with no return to Sly and the Hostess, and so has the last laugh on those who wish to see it as just another example of the shrew-taming genre. It is easier to appreciate this when the play is compared with a sequel written by John Fletcher, *The Woman's Prize or the Tamer Tamed* (1611). This begins with Petruchio's second wedding, this time to Bianca, who sets out to take revenge on Petruchio for what he did to Kate. She and her friends lock him out of the upstairs bedroom, defending it like a castle from invaders. But the right she claims is the freedom to spend his money without restraint. In the end he resorts to feigning death in order to bring her back in line. An epilogue states that the play seeks 'To teach both sexes due equality', and a production directed by Greg Doran for the RSC in 2004 was advertised as a feminist answer to Shakespeare's play. But the phrase 'due equality' here is relative, and simply signifies the restoration of traditional male/female relations, rather than equality as we now understand the term. Shakespeare's work, by contrast, gets under the skin; it makes people argue. It attempts to use the power of theatre to subvert a hoary social problem. It may not be entirely successful in this endeavour, but it is a very early play, and Kate is the first in a long line of outspoken Shakespearean heroines.

The Merchant of Venice

The transfer of David Thacker's production of *The Merchant of Venice* for the RSC to the Barbican Theatre, London, on April 4 1994 was marked in the *Guardian* newspaper with a dialogue between Thacker and the Jewish dramatist Arnold Wesker. Their argument – part of an ongoing campaign by this dramatist against the play – focused inevitably on the question of anti-Semitism but also skirted around a central problem of theatrical criticism:

the question of when interpretation becomes rewriting, and the circumstances in which that is desirable or even legitimate.

Wesker has himself rewritten the play: *The Merchant* (1977). His adaptation uses the same story line as Shakespeare's, but his Shylock and Antonio are the best of friends, and the merry bond is simply a foolhardy attempt to cock a snook at Venetian laws forbidding informal financial transactions between Venetian citizens and the inhabitants of the Jewish ghetto. Wesker's complaint about Thacker's production was that in attempting to present Shakespeare's Shylock as a cultured, intelligent man, deeply aware of the way in which his life was circumvented by his racial origin, it was being dishonest. Thacker agreed with him – 'You're absolutely right. It's dishonest in that it is subverting the text' – and his production had in fact cut 200 lines of text while rearranging some others.

The stage history of Shakespeare's play can be divided between those productions which have sought to present a sympathetic Shylock, and those which have gone all out for the monster. Andrew Manley's production for the Harrogate Theatre, Yorkshire, also in 1994, was deeply conscious of this second tradition: the usurer with hideous nose and red ear-locked wig who might almost be seen as a validation by Shakespeare of Nazi ideology. Although there was virtually no additional dialogue, Shakespeare's play became a play-within-a-play, in which the audience were cast in the roles of perpetrators of, or at the very least passive participants in, anti-Semitism. The gilded, late Victorian auditorium of the theatre was for the first half swathed in institutional, laundry-marked sheets as we, along with the guards of a Nazi concentration camp, played by members of the Harrogate youth theatre, watched a group of Jewish inmates rehearsing a production. The group's *Capo*, in the role of both Antonio and stage director, kept one anxious eye on the reactions of the guards, while driving his fellow prisoner playing Shylock to act with ever greater excesses of

Jewish caricature. The second half of the play became the actual camp performance. The sheets were whipped away, the guards occupied the stage boxes and the cast appeared in full traditional doublet and hose costuming against a theatrical box set.

At one point in the 'rehearsal' section, the starving prisoners had watched mesmerised as one of the guards ostentatiously ate an apple. Having delivered the 'If you prick us, do we not bleed' speech (3.1.50–62), Shylock (Damien Myerscough) attacked him. The *Capo* pulled him off and the 'rehearsal' continued, but in the 'performance', as Shylock turned for his final exit, the guard calmly lifted his revolver and shot him dead, centre stage. Terror ensured that the remaining prisoners in the cast could do nothing but continue, and the Belmont scene was played with the characters stepping around the body, being careful not to look at it. The effect of this on us as audience was highly disturbing, since we no longer knew what the outcome would be. Would the production end in further executions? Shakespeare's play came to its curtain call and we applauded, but the staging meant that we were unsure whether we were clapping the Harrogate actors as ourselves, or the Jewish prisoners as members of the SS. The guards left their boxes but we all remained in our seats in the lit auditorium, the dead body still protruding from under the act drop, waiting for something else to happen. Eventually we straggled out of the theatre, aware that our play – our response to what we had seen – was still going on.

It was an immensely powerful production that I read as using the play to confront anti-Semitic prejudice. The director's rationale, however, was:

> to take the holocaust head-on and the classic way of doing that is to do a sympathetic Shylock. But Shylock is meant to be a villain, like a pantomime villain and Shakespeare thought it a wheeze to make him Jewish. If you go for a sympathetic Shylock you emasculate the play.

But why would Shakespeare want to present a villainous Jew?
There had been no overtly practising Jews in England since the
expulsion of 1290, although small, fluctuating groups of
converted Jews lived in London and Bristol, mostly refugees of
the Inquisition in Spain and Portugal. The word 'Jew', however,
was often used synonymously with 'usurer', as in this typically
robust satire by Nashe on the abuses of life in London:

> When a legion of devils ... were cast forth of two men that
> came out of graves, they desired they might go into hogs or
> swine (which are usurers,) ... The Jews were all hogs, that is
> usurers, and therefore if there had been no divine restraint for
> it, yet nature itself would have dissuaded them from eating
> swine's flesh, that is from feeding on one another. The prodi-
> gal child in the Gospel is reported to have fed hogs, that is,
> usurers, by letting them beguile him of his substance.
>
> (Thomas Nashe, *Christ's Tears Over Jerusalem*,
> 1593, pp. 49–50)

We still use the phrase 'snouts in the trough' to denote financial
greed and exploitation, but capitalism, which was nascent in the
later sixteenth century, cannot function without money-
lending, and lending money at interest was prohibited by the
tenets of Christian faith, as it is still prohibited in Islamic law.
The Act Against Usury in 1571 clarified the situation. Interest
could be charged to a maximum of ten per cent The previous
year Shakespeare's father had been prosecuted twice, accused of
lending money at the extortionate rates of twenty and twenty-
five per cent.

In 1994, David Thacker's production, with its steel and glass
setting evocative of the money market, did not convince all the
critics, perhaps because, as Robert Hanks noted in the
Independent, 'an aversion to money-lending is not exactly rife in
such a milieu' (11 April 1994), but perhaps more because he was

concentrating so hard on not being anti-Semitic. It is rarely
noticed that Shylock's pound of flesh is a law of Christian
Venice, and no more unreasonable *in the market* than the
Venetian practice of keeping slaves:

> You have among you many a purchased slave,
> Which, like your asses and your dogs and mules,
> You use in abject and in slavish parts
> Because you bought them. Shall I say to you
> 'Let them be free, marry them to your heirs'?
>   … You will answer
> 'The slaves are ours.' So do I answer you.
> 'The pound of flesh which I demand of him
> Is dearly bought. 'Tis mine, and I will have it.'
> If you deny me, fie upon your law,
> There is no force in the decrees of Venice.
>   (4.1.90–102)

Shakespeare's play tackles a difficult contemporary moral and
legal issue in which he and his family were implicated. In the
intervening four hundred years, the course of history has
changed our perception and an aspect of the play which was at
least in part a metaphor for the operation of the market – usurer
as Jew – has become in criticism of the play simply 'Jew'. But
while our pensions and interest-bearing cheque accounts ensure
that everyone in the developed world has a stake in Shylockery,
we are still not able to balance wealth creation with equity and
justice. We do not even all agree it would be desirable.

Struggles for economic and political power are often encap-
sulated in racial or religious difference, and there is scope for
interpreting the play now in this way. Indeed the director Peter
Sellars has partly done so, also in 1994, with a production in
which Shylock, an African American, and Portia, a Chinese
American, performed in front of banks of TV screens that
alternated images of fabulously wealthy California real estate

with footage of the beating of the black man Rodney King by the Los Angeles police, and the subsequent riots.

Conclusion: worldwide Shakespeare

In the spring of 2010 in Romania, the seventh Craiova International Shakespeare Festival was devoted entirely to *Hamlet*. The play had performed the role of midwife at the birth of the present post-communist state in 1989 in a production by the Bulandra Theatre, in which Claudius and Gertrude had been presented as scarcely veiled portraits of the communist dictator Nicolae Ceauşescu and his wife. It had performed to packed houses in Bucharest for six months prior to the revolution, and Ion Caramitru, who played Hamlet, would subsequently become Minister for Culture in the new government.

Careful attention had been paid to the translation, with passages culled from all the existing Romanian translations as a way of distracting the censors' attention from certain newly translated sections, and from the political message of the production overall. Fortinbras's line 'go bid the soldiers shoot' was the cue to machine-gun everyone on the stage, as it was in Ingmar Bergman's production in Sweden in 1986. In the light of the military dictatorships of the twentieth century, it seemed inevitable that Hamlet's notorious inaction should result in further repression.

But in the twenty years since the break-up of the Soviet Union and the end of the Cold War, identity politics has taken over from politics. Of the ten productions that came to Craiova from all over the world – China, Japan, Lithuania, Poland, Germany, Romania, and the USA as well as Britain – all but one had cut Fortinbras entirely. Identity of course becomes particularly important for countries that have only recently gained independence. The Lithuanian production from the

Vilnius City Theatre accordingly fastened on the opening line of the play: 'Who's there?' Its set consisted of a number of identical dressing tables – the symbol of the actor's craft of make-up and make-believe – which were furiously wheeled about in endless different permutations, both during and between scenes. It was Gertrude who held the skull in front of one of these mirrors, thus staging Hamlet's line 'get you to my lady's chamber, and tell her, let her paint an inch thick, to this favour she must come' (5.1.190–1). In dialogue after the show, the director, Oskaras Koršunovas, admitted that he saw himself in Hamlet.

The production from the Schaubühne in Berlin directed by Thomas Ostermeier has performed to huge acclaim round the world. It doubled Ophelia and Gertrude, with the Gertrude character performing for Hamlet's video camera as celebrity singer, 'wife and girlfriend'. Denmark was both grave, and indulgent banquet, with tons of earth on the stage, and a long table on rollers that stretched across its width, and which became increasingly strewn with detritus. It played for two and a half hours, without an interval. Lars Eidinger, a tall, slim, and athletic actor, wore a fat suit with beer gut, and gave an astounding performance as a slovenly Hamlet with Tourette's syndrome, which captured the idea, present in Shakespeare's play, but often overlooked, of Hamlet as clown. Shocking and bloody, the production was also on occasion very funny. Eidinger often engaged directly with the audience, and there was some added repartee in English, the *lingua franca*, designed specifically for the Romanian context.

In the Japanese Ryutopia Noh Theatre Shakespeare Company production, Hirokazu Kouchi as Hamlet remained seated cross-legged on stage throughout – a remarkable feat of physical endurance, which became almost painful to watch. Whenever the words demanded physical action, a trio of actors using the traditional gestures of Japanese theatre moved in behind him. It was as if he himself was telling his tale 'aright' to the world, as he asks

Horatio to do at the end of the play. Perhaps uniquely in the history of *Hamlet* productions, there was no skull, no Yorick, but it referred not once but three times to the story of Pyrrhus.

Each of these productions was a meditation on a selected *theme* of *Hamlet*. Each achieved some astounding theatrical effects and was stylistically modern and arresting. But each, in its different way, had cut the play to focus on Hamlet as an individual troubled soul, a performance tradition that dates from the influence of early nineteenth-century romanticism.

It is sometimes claimed by British theatre critics that foreign language Shakespeare tends to be more theatrically successful than performance in English because it is freed from the requirement to speak Shakespeare's actual words: it is usually heavily cut, and translated using modern idioms. Yet, as Ion Caramitru proudly pointed out in Craiova, Romanian is the sole European language that can translate 'To be or not to be' using the same vowel sounds and rhythm as in English. More than twenty years on from his seminal performance in the role, he performed that speech, in Romanian, as part of a public discussion of the play, clearly intensely alive to its nuances, its shades of doubt, and its contradictions.

Since Shakespeare's stories are borrowed from other, often forgotten authors, it follows that the essence of what we value in Shakespeare lies in the structures he gives to those stories, and in his language – its shapes and sounds, and the way it can introduce a startling new image or change direction mid line. The challenge, and the opportunity, for English speakers is therefore to perform the plays of Shakespeare with the same sense of freedom and vigour that we often find in non-English Shakespeare, reinventing them for modern audiences, while doing justice to their complex, discursive structures in both plot and language. It is these open structures – the contrast of characters, the puns, the repetition-with-difference – that allow both audiences and readers the freedom to feel, think, and imagine.

Further reading

All sixteenth- and seventeenth-century printed texts are in Early English Books Online (http://eebo.chadwyck.com). I have modernised the spelling and punctuation of all quotations, and keyed quotations from Shakespeare to the Alexander edition (Collins, 1951, and frequently reprinted).

Introduction: Why Shakespeare?

Accurate plot summaries of all Shakespeare's plays can be found in Michael Dobson and Stanley Wells, *The Oxford Companion to Shakespeare* (Oxford University Press, 2001) and online in the Literary Encyclopedia http://www.litencyc.com. The Shakespeare Handbooks series (Palgrave Macmillan) provides extensive commentaries and critical analysis of individual plays. Books on Elizabethan religion and politics include Andrew Hadfield, *Shakespeare and Republicanism* (Cambridge University Press, 2005). For the political importance of early modern drama, see Kent Cartwright, *Theatre and Humanism* (Cambridge University Press, 1999), and Greg Walker, *The politics of Performance in Early Renaissance Drama* (Cambridge University Press, 1998).

Chapter 1: Who, and what, is Shakespeare?

Shakespeare's will and other personal records are reproduced in S. Schoenbaum, *William Shakespeare: A Documentary Life*

(Clarendon Press, 1975). Michael Dobson tells how Shakespeare became a national icon in *The Making of the National Poet* (Clarendon Press, 1992). James Shapiro, who presents a fascinating micro-study of one year in his life in *1599* (Faber and Faber, 2005), refutes claims that Shakespeare was not responsible for the plays that go by his name in *Contested Will: Who Wrote Shakespeare?* (Simon and Schuster, 2010).

T.W. Baldwin's, *William Shakespere's Small Latine and Lesse Greeke* (University of Illinois, 1944) analyses sixteenth-century grammar school education, while E.R.J. Honigmann's, *Shakespeare, the 'Lost Years'* (Manchester University Press, 1985) examines the suggestion that Shakespeare was a schoolmaster in Lancashire.

Scott McMillin and Sally-Beth McLean provide a comprehensive account of the *Queen's Men and their Plays* (Cambridge University Press, 1998). For further details on the late plays and court performances, see Ros King, *The Winter's Tale* (Palgrave Macmillan, 2008) and *Cymbeline: Constructions of Britain* (Ashgate, 2005). Portraits of Shakespeare are discussed by Tarnya Cooper (ed.), *Searching for Shakespeare* (National Portrait Gallery and Yale University Press, 2006).

The standard accounts of theatres in Elizabethan London are by Andrew Gurr: *The Shakespearean Stage* (Cambridge University Press, 1970); *Playgoing in Shakespeare's London* (Cambridge University Press, 1987), both subsequently revised and reprinted. Julian Bowsher and Pat Miller report on the archaeology of the London theatre sites in *The Rose and the Globe – playhouses of Shakespeare's Bankside, Southwark: Excavations 1988–90* (Museum of London Archaeology, 2009).

Jonson in *Every Man out of his Humour*, Barnabe Barnes in *The Devil's Charter*, and John Webster in *The Duchess of Malfi* all claim on the title pages that the printed editions contain 'more than hath been publickely spoken or acted', leading Lucas Erne in *Shakespeare as Literary Dramatist* (Cambridge University Press,

2003) to claim that Shakespeare wrote for print. The most clear-sighted of short articles on the printing of Shakespeare's plays is Peter W.M. Blayney, 'The Publication of Playbooks', in John D. Cox and David Scott Kastan (eds), *A New History of Early English Drama* (Columbia University Press, 1997). Some of the implications of the differences between Q and F *King Lear* are discussed by the contributors to *The Division of the Kingdoms* (ed. Gary Taylor, Clarendon Press, 1983).

Chapter 2: Shakespeare and the theatre business

Documents, both official and theatrical, relating to plays and playing were collected and discussed by E.K. Chambers in *The Elizabethan Stage* (4 vols, Clarendon Press, 1923). There is an ongoing project by *Records of Early English Drama* (Toronto) to edit and print all references to play and music performance in each English county and in Scotland and Wales. All references to Henslowe's accounts can be found in R.A. Foakes and R.T. Rickert, *Henslowe's Diary* (Cambridge University Press, 1961). Andrew Gurr provides a history of the Admiral's Men in *Shakespeare's Opposites* (Cambridge University Press, 2009).

Three books by Tiffany Stern give an invaluable account of theatre practices in the period: *Rehearsal from Shakespeare to Sheridan* (Clarendon Press, 2000); *Shakespeare in Parts* (with Simon Palfrey; Oxford University Press, 2007); and *Documents of Performance in Early Modern England* (Cambridge University Press, 2009).

Stylistic analysis of the possible collaborative authorship of some of Shakespeare's plays can be found in Hugh Craig and Arthur F. Kinney (eds), *Shakespeare, Computers and the Mystery of Authorship* (Cambridge University Press, 2009), and Brian Vickers, *Shakespeare, Co-Author* (Oxford University Press, 2002).

Further analysis of *The Comedy of Errors* and the performance at Gray's Inn is in Ros King's updated edition of T.S. Dorsch (ed.), *The Comedy of Errors* (Cambridge University Press, 2004).

Chapter 3: Shakespeare's structures: plot, genre, and character

The major sources that Shakespeare used in his plays are gathered together in the seven volumes of Geoffrey Bullough's *Narrative and Dramatic Sources of Shakespeare* (Routledge, 1957–75). For play construction, see David Edgar's helpful analysis *How Plays Work* (Nick Hern Books, 2009). T.W. Baldwin explores renaissance theories of five-act structure in *Shakespeare's Five Act Structure* (University of Illinois Press, 1947); John Wilders looks at the relationship between history and tragedy in *The Lost Garden* (Macmillan, 1978); and John Jones examines revision in *Shakespeare at Work* (Clarendon, 1995). F.S. Boas coined the term 'problem play' in *Shakespeare and his Predecessors* (Murray, 1896), while C.L. Barber was responsible for *Shakespeare's Festive Comedy* (Princeton, 1959, 1972). Bertrand Evans uses 'discrepant awareness' in *Shakespeare's Comedies* (Clarendon Press, 1960). M.M. Mahood explores the importance of minor roles in *Playing Bit Parts in Shakespeare* (Routledge, 1998; first published as *Bit Parts in Shakespeare's Plays*, Cambridge University Press, 1992).

The Oxford don's description of Desdemona was printed in the *Times Literary Supplement*, 20 July 1933.

Chapter 4: Reading, hearing, and seeing Shakespeare

Anthony Corbeill's study of gesture in the classical world is in *Nature Embodied* (Princeton, 2004). Modern study of the relationship between gesture, thought, and language began with David McNeil's *Hand and Mind* (University of Chicago, 1992). See also Antonio Damasio, *The Feeling of What Happens* (Vintage, 2000).

For knowledge and use of classical memory techniques in the early modern world, see Frances Yates, *The Art of Memory* (Routledge, 1966), and Mary Carruthers, *The Book of Memory* (Cambridge University Press, 1990).

Definitions of rhetorical terms can be found at http://rhetoric.byu.edu/. Stephen Booth's edition of the sonnets was published by Yale University Press (1977 and 2000), and Jonathan Hope's *Shakespeare's Grammar* by Arden Shakespeare (2003).

The Elizabethan sound world is explored by Bruce R. Smith, *The Acoustic World of Early Modern England* (University of Chicago, 1999). Books on music include David Lindley, *Shakespeare and Music* (Thomson, 2006); and Ross W. Duffin, *Shakespeare's Songbook* (Norton, 2004), which prints suitable song and ballad tunes for the songs in Shakespeare. On metrics and verse form see George T. Wright, *Shakespeare's Metrical Art* (University of California, 1988), and Philip Hobsbaum, *Metre, Rhythm, and Verse Form* (Routledge, 1996).

Chapter 5: Interpreting Shakespeare

Through the technique of selective quotation, *Shakespeare in Charge* (Little, Brown and Co, 1999) by Norman Augustine and Kenneth Adelman mines Shakespeare's plays for 'lessons' in management and leadership. Adelman is a former US ambassador and enthusiastic supporter of the war in Iraq. Like Adelman, Richard Olivier, who directed *Henry V* for the Shakespeare's Globe opening season (1997), runs a training company for business managers using Shakespeare's plays as an instruction tool. See Diana E. Henderson, 'Meditations in a Time of (Displaced) War' in Ros King and Paul J.C.M. Franssen (eds), *Shakespeare and War* (Palgrave Macmillan, 2008).

Jan Kott's *Shakespeare Our Contemporary* (Methuen, 1965) was hugely influential in twentieth-century politically motivated productions and criticism. Lawyer Theodor Meron is the author of a number of books on Shakespeare's knowledge of just war theory, including *Shakespeare's Wars and Shakespeare's Laws* (Clarendon Press, 1993). See also Nick de Simogyi, *Shakespeare's Theatre of War* (Ashgate, 1998), and Ros King and Paul J.C.M. Franssen (eds), *Shakespeare and War* (Palgrave Macmillan, 2008). James Shapiro considers *Shakespeare and the Jews* (Columbia University Press, 1996), and John Gross, *Shylock: a Legend and its Legacy* (Simon and Schuster, 1994).

Arnold Wesker's *The Merchant* is available in various collections of twentieth-century drama, and in a student edition (Methuen Drama, 1983).

Index

A Beginner's Guide to Aquinas

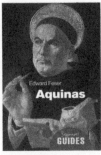

9781851686902
£9.99/ $14.95

St Thomas Aquinas established the foundations for much of modern philosophy of religion, and is infamous for his arguments for the existence of God. Covering his thoughts on the soul, natural law, metaphysics, and the interaction of faith and reason, this will prove a indispensible resource for students, experts or the general reader.

"A useful and easy to read introduction. Students and scholars will find [this] highly beneficial." **Fulvio di Blasi,** President, Thomas International

"Lucid, cogent, and compelling. Required reading for anyone interested in Thomas Aquinas." **Christopher Kaczor,** Associate Professor of Philosophy, Loyola Marymount University

Edward Feser is Visiting Assistant Professor of Philosophy at Loyola Marymount University, California. He is the author of *Locke*.

A Beginner's Guide to Classical Music

9781851686872
£9.99/ $14.95

What does classical music mean to the Western World? How has it transformed over the centuries? With such a rich tradition, what relevance does it have today? Julian Johnson inspires readers to explore the field, and examines how music is related to some of the big ideas of Western experience, including spirituality, emotion, the weight of history, and self identity.

"Johnson combines boundless enthusiasm for the subject with extensive knowledge and manages to convey a decent quantity of the latter in economical and effortless fashion."
Classical Music

JULIAN JOHNSON is Professor of Music at Royal Holloway, University of London. He is also a composer and speaker on musicology, championing the relevance of classical music to the general public.

Browse further titles at
www.oneworld-publications.com

A Beginner's Guide to The Enlightenment

9781851687091
£9.99/ $14.95

The Enlightenment has been nothing if not divisive. To this day historians disagree over when it was, where it was, and what it was. Kieron O'Hara traverses these conflicts, presenting the history, politics, science, religion, arts, and social life of the Enlightenment not as a simple set of easily enumerated ideas, but an evolving conglomerate that spawned a very diverse set of thinkers.

"Thorough without ever being forbidding." **Dan Hind**, author of *The Threat to Reason: How the Enlightenment Was Hijacked and How We Can Reclaim It*

"Engaging and highly readable." **Matthew Humphrey**, Reader in Political Philosophy, University of Nottingham

"Excellent and remarkably comprehensive" **Penny Fielding**, Senior Lecturer in English Literature, University of Edinburgh

KIERON O'HARA is a Senior Researcher at Southampton University. He is the author of *The Spy in the Coffee Machine: The End of Privacy as We Know It* (also Oneworld), *Trust: From Socrates to Spin*, and *After Blair: David Cameron and the Conservative Tradition*.

Browse further titles at
www.oneworld-publications.com

A Beginner's Guide to Renaissance Art

9781851687244
£9.99/ $14.95

The fifteenth century saw the evolution of a distinct and powerfully influential European artistic culture. But what does the familiar phrase "Renaissance Art" actually refer to? Through engaging discussion of timeless works by artists such as Jan van Eyck, Leonardo da Vinci, and Michelangelo, Tom Nichols offers a masterpiece of his own as he explores the truly original and diverse character of the art of the Renaissance.

"Expertly informed and highly readable." **Peter Humfrey**, Professor of Art History, University of St Andrews

"Exceptionally informative... and articulated in a way that is remarkably fresh." **Malcolm Bull**, The Ruskin School of Drawing and Fine Art, University of Oxford, and Andrew W. Mellon Visiting Professor, The Courtauld Institute of Art

"An excellent introduction" **Tania String**, Senior Lecturer in History of Art, University of Bristol

TOM NICHOLS is Senior Lecturer in History of Art at the University of Aberdeen. His recent publications include *The Art of Poverty, Tintoretto, Tradition and Identity*, and *Others and Outcasts in Early Modern Europe*.

Browse further titles at
www.oneworld-publications.com

A Beginner's Guide to Machiavelli

9781851686391
£9.99/ $14.95

Machiavelli has been among the most commented upon, criticized and feared thinkers of the modern world. Infamous for his support of brutality and repression as valid political instruments, he is often portrayed as the pantomime villain of political theorists. Nederman highlights the complexities in his thought, showing that he actually advocated democracy as much as dictatorship, debate as much as violence, depending upon prevailing political conditions.

"Nederman persuasively illuminates the power and complexity of the Florentine's political thought." Mary Dietz, Professor of Political Science, University of Minnesota

"A fresh approach to Machiavelli that explains many of the puzzles in his writings. " John Christian Laursen, Professor of Political Science, University of California at Riverside

CARY J. NEDERMAN is professor of political science at Texas A&M University. He is the author of over twenty books on the history of Western political thought.

Browse further titles at
www.oneworld-publications.com